P9-DMG-115

TEACHING READING
COMPREHENSION
AND VOCABULARY

TEACHING READING COMPREHENSION AND VOCABULARY

A GUIDE FOR TEACHERS

Marvin L. Klein
Western Washington University

PRENTICE HALL, Englewood Cliffs, New Jersey 07632

Library of Congress Cataloging-in-Publication Data

Klein, Marvin L.
  Teaching reading comprehension and vocabulary.

  Includes bibliographies and index.
  1. Reading comprehension — Study and teaching.
  2. Vocabulary — Study and teaching. I. Title.
LB1050.45.K54 1988   428.4'3'07   87-32848
ISBN 0-13-895293-0

Editorial/production supervision and
  interior design: Merrill Peterson
Cover design: Ben Santora
Manufacturing buyer: Margaret Rizzi

© 1988 by Prentice-Hall, Inc.
A Division of Simon & Schuster
Englewood Cliffs, New Jersey 07632

Printed in the United States of America

10 9 8 7 6 5 4 3 2

ISBN 0-13-895293-0   01

Prentice-Hall International (UK) Limited, *London*
Prentice-Hall of Australia Pty. Limited, *Sydney*
Prentice-Hall Canada Inc., *Toronto*
Prentice-Hall Hispanoamericana, S.A., *Mexico*
Prentice-Hall of India Private Limited, *New Delhi*
Prentice-Hall of Japan, Inc., *Tokyo*
Simon & Schuster Asia Pte. Ltd., *Singapore*
Editora Prentice-Hall do Brasil, Ltda., *Rio de Janeiro*

Contents

3   TEACHING READING VOCABULARY   59

4   SELF-MONITORING   93

5   THE READING/WRITING CONNECTION   116

6   TEACHING TEXT STRUCTURE AND ORGANIZATION   132

7   BASAL READERS   151

8   EPILOGUE   161

Preface

Reading instruction has come a long way in the past two decades. In the last decade alone it has advanced perhaps more than in all those preceding in this century. Especially important are advances in the areas of reading comprehension and vocabulary development. We have learned more about the reading act, the processes of reading, and the relationship of reader and text than ever before.

In addition, reading educators have given increased priority to reading comprehension and vocabulary development as critical components of the reading program. During the past eight to ten years a number of major studies in the area of comprehension have been completed and reported. During that same period a number of specialized books on reading comprehension have been published. Most of these books have been concerned with elaborating newer theories of reading comprehension and providing analyses and summaries of the research. A few have suggested possible activities which derive from that body of literature.

In the early days of this book's inception, it was seen as a similar publication on reading comprehension and vocabulary. However, it became increasingly clear with the appearance of a number of excellent books which did that sort of thing, that another was not warranted. Instead, what was needed was a guide for teachers, a guide whose roots were in reading comprehension and vocabulary research and theory, but whose primary goal was to provide teachers with both a summary of key theory and research in these areas and a selection of strategies, techniques, and activities that could serve as instructional models for any reading program and at most grade levels.

It is hoped that this book can serve a useful role in teacher preparation programs, teacher in-service, and other similar settings. It is intended to be an ongoing resource handbook which should wear well with time and which can serve as a companion in a variety of teaching contexts and conditions.

Chapter One examines briefly some of the contemporary history of reading instruction development, some of the conceptual and definitional issues which have plagued reading educators over the years, and some of the key research and theory that have been central to the development of approaches to reading comprehension and vocabulary instruction.

Chapter Two focuses upon questioning and its role in improving reading comprehension. Discussion of the nature of questioning strategies is followed by an elaboration of selected questioning strategies and suggestions for their exploitation.

Chapter Three addresses reading vocabulary as an instructional component in the reading program. Identification of vocabulary *dictionaries* and their various roles precedes an elaboration of different direct instructional strategies and an array of techniques and activities for improving reading vocabulary instruction.

Chapter Four explores *self-monitoring* as a metacognitive operation. Its importance to the reading program is discussed and a wide selection of techniques and activities for incorporating self-monitoring approaches into the reading program are presented.

Chapter Five focuses upon the reading/writing connection. It considers the relationship of the two and makes a conceptual distinction between writing-as-supplement and writing-as-integral to the reading program. A number of approaches for incorporating writing into the reading program are offered.

Chapter Six is devoted to the structure and organization of the text. Techniques and activities presented here are designed to get students directly involved with the structure of text so that they control it more than it controls them.

Chapter Seven examines the role of basal readers in the teaching of comprehension and reading vocabulary.

Chapter Eight concludes the book with a brief treatment of key ideas important for a total reading program in order to have effective reading comprehension and vocabulary development.

The Preface remains one of the few places where an author can offer proper gratitude to a few of the people who were helpful in a book's production. Because the list is typically substantial, singling out only a few of those who played an important role is very difficult.

My wife, Kay, played a dominant professional role serving as ongoing critic and editor. Her helpful ideas for both content and format have made this a better book than it would have been without her. Her love, care, and understanding, however, were the most critical elements to the completion of the project. Thanks to Meredith for her patience and tolerance. The project robbed the family of some time together. She understood. Thanks to George Lamb, friend and professional critic, for his assistance in developing this book. Judy Kramer and others in the Bureau for Faculty Research at Western Washington University worked hard in the preparation of final manuscript. Thanks to all of them.

As usual, Shirley Chlopak and others at Prentice Hall have provided necessary professional guidance and direction. Candace Demeduc assisted tremendously as an excellent copy editor. And I must also thank Susan Willig for her support of this project as well as others at Prentice Hall with whom I have been fortunate enough to be involved.

Finally, thanks to my many colleagues and to outside reviewers who helped make this a far better book than it would have been otherwise. I appreciate their helpful comments and advice along the way and, of course, burden none of them with any faults that might remain.

Marvin L. Klein

TEACHING READING COMPREHENSION AND VOCABULARY

1

Reading Comprehension

AN IDEA WHOSE TIME HAS COME

New teachers might find it difficult to believe that our current interest in reading comprehension instruction did not always exist. Yet, prior to the 1970s, many educators wondered whether something like comprehension could even be taught. Comprehension was so global in nature that it defied our ability to identify its most salient features with enough specificity and confidence to include it in our curriculum.

This is not to suggest that the ability to comprehend what we read was viewed as unimportant, for it clearly was. We simply could not get a good enough grip on the idea to design instructional approaches which assured its development.

Even by the 1930s and 1940s there was substantial interest in a variety of factors which were related to reading comprehension. For example, studies in text readability were done by Gray and Leary in 1935 and by Lorge in 1939. Factor analytic studies by Davis et al. in the 1940s and beyond attempted to resolve some of the disputes about whether there were, indeed, *specie-specific* factors characteristic of reading comprehension.* And, as most reading scholars know, as early as 1908 Huey introduced important ideas about comprehension as a product and, more importantly, as a process.

However, for whatever reasons, from the 1950s through the early 1970s most of our attention in reading instruction focused upon decoding and its role in the reading program. Possible impetus for this focus came from a variety of sources. The comparative ease of identifying critical decoding skills as opposed to identifying comprehension skills was one reason. Another was the arrival on the scene in the late 1950s and early 1960s of linguistics as a science—old and respected in the traditional academic world of the humanities, but relatively new and intriguing to reading educators. Beginning in the 1960s, *linguistic readers* began to gain part of the basal reader market, and they warranted considerable attention in the well-known "First Grade Studies" (Bond and Dykstra, 1967). Premised primarily upon the assumptions of structural linguistics rather than the brash young linguistic baby-on-the-block—transformational grammar— these linguistic readers focused almost entirely upon sound-symbol relationships in a tightly ordered fashion. Often even pictures were discouraged since they distracted the reader from the text itself.

Also, in 1967 Chall's *Learning to Read: The Great Debate* appeared. Many interpreted Chall's analysis of the contemporary condition of reading instruction to advocate that more attention be paid to phonics.

All of these factors converged at a time in our history when there was a national decline in test scores and a major push at the federal level for emphasizing basic skills in the schools—how these skills were defined changed quite dramatically through the 1970s.

The emphasis on decoding was reinforced by commercially published basal reading programs during this period. It must be remembered that basal reading series command the overwhelming majority of all school reading programs. Reasonable estimates suggest that they serve as the base for the reading program in 90% to 95% of all schools, K–6. We also know that of all textbooks sold for education in kindergarten through college, basal readers constitute just under 40% of the total. Estimates place total K–8 basal reading textbook sales for 1985 at over $314 million. Basal readers clearly play an important role in our reading programs throughout the United States.

Through the latter 1970s these programs reflected a continued emphasis upon phonics instruction, especially in the early grades, although in some programs this instruction continued through the intermediate and

---

*Word difficulty and reasoning were the two independent factors that appeared to surface consistently.

middle school years. We can note differences in both degree of emphasis, from nearly total to more moderate, and in methodology of instruction, from synthetic to analytic. Regardless of difference, however, we can find certain commonalities in these programs. They clearly placed a fundamental emphasis upon phonics instruction in the K–2 grades with little or no attention given to comprehension at those levels. These programs were based on the belief that comprehension does not or cannot take place until decoding skills are mastered. In fact, it was commonly asserted during this period that an orderly sequence of skill categories was from decoding to comprehension to study skills to reading to enjoyment.

The issue of whether basal reading programs are at the forefront in implementing new ideas or whether they simply reflect the ongoing demands and practices of the market is a moot one. They certainly do substantially reflect the practical translation of reading research and theory.

By the latter 1960s and early 1970s, new ideas were shaping the direction of reading instruction. The new transformational grammar and so-called *case grammars* enticed reading researchers into the arena of sentence meaning; bands of hearty followers eager to expand the boundaries of reading interests searched for research approaches using these new linguistic tools. Reading educators found themselves in the company of cognitive and developmental psychologists, linguists, psycholinguists (those studying the relation of language to thought and its development in children), sociologists, and even anthropologists. The role of cognitive processes present in the act of reading gained more attention. The structure and sound of the language *per se* seemed of less importance than did the role of language as an abstracting system important in comprehension.

After at least a decade of attention, decoding instruction was not significantly improving overall reading scores. In the latter 1960s, the first nationwide assessments began, and by the mid-1970s there were indications from the data of the National Assesment of Educational Progress (NAEP) that basic skills in reading—word-attack skills generally—were improving in the lower-level achievers. Unfortunately, throughout the decade of the 1970s, scores in reading comprehension—especially in areas requiring higher-level inferential skills—declined or failed to improve. The most significant declines took place in the top 25% of learners. In the 1979–1980 assessment, NAEP reported that any improvements in comprehension were restricted to younger students, and the declines in comprehension continued in older and more academically talented students. Whatever else was going on in our reading programs, comprehension was not being developed.

There were two major research shifts during the 1970s that brought us into the 1980s on a significantly new note. One was the development of approaches to text analysis based upon the larger *grammars* or structures underpinning text longer than sentences.* An example of this sort of textual analysis can be seen in Halliday and Hasan's "cohesion theory" (1976). Halliday and Hasan showed how text coheres in a variety of ways. More common cohesive ties are pronouns, their referents, and their system of reference. Other ties are made through grammatical structures. Semantic or meaning ties are made through word collocations, i.e., topic and descriptive words establish a *word family context* whereby the presence of one word or word type attracts others to the text. For example, if we had a text about life in a pond, it is quite likely that words such as *water, sand, lily-pad, shore,* and so on are going to appear somewhere in the text.

The Halliday and Hasan model was *text-bound* in the sense that its focus was not on the reader but on language in print. As linguists, Halliday and Hasan logically brought a language-centered perspective to their work. During the latter 1970s considerable research in reading comprehension was conducted using the cohesive-ties model. Typically, two near-identical contrived texts were presented to subjects with alterations made in the cohesive ties of one version only. For example, the basic content of a short passage was held constant in the control text while the distance between referential ties, such as pronouns, was manipulated in the altered experimental text. Findings suggested, among other things, that the greater the referential-tie distance, the more difficult the comprehension of the text.

During the same period, Nancy Stein developed a variety of *story grammars*—the hierarchy of structural and content relationships which hold within well-formed stories (Stein and Glenn, 1979). For example, Stein observed, along with many anthropologists, sociologists, and philosophers such as Claude Levi-Strauss, that there appear to be universal elements such as setting, initiating event, character development, problem, problem resolution, climax, denouement, and so on that recur in all well-formed stories. One might even postulate that this universality suggests characteristics innate to authors of stories and is, therefore, implicit in readers—a tacit set of literary structures, if you will.

Conceptual and psychological arguments aside, most of the story grammar approaches started as text-bound models, and, some would assert, they remain as such. Stein's work in the mid-70s represented an effort to find some kinds of correspondence between story structure and reading processing.

In some respects, this was the same driving imperative that was behind the interesting theoretical model proposed by Walter Kintsch (1974). His *propositional networks* model attempted to formulate the relationships that drive the structure and content of certain kinds of nonfiction text and which give the researcher an indication of the processing properties involved during the reading act (Kintsch and Van Dijk, 1978).

*Sometimes called *text macrostructures*.

The work of Kintsch and Stein in the mid-70s represents the transition of reading scholars from the examination of the complexity of language and its components in text to an increasing interest in the reading process, i.e., what goes on in the reader during the reading act.

This interest was reflected also in research in communications theory expansion, artificial intelligence, and computer-assisted approaches to reading research. Several theory and research-directed models were developed during the 1970s (Rumelhart, 1977).*

By the latter 1970s, however, contemporary reading scholars increasingly moved away from the text *per se* and towards the reader as processor of text.

The 1970s saw the incorporation of ideas from the newer linguistics, which suggested at least that it could answer questions not only about the structure and semantic character of text—in both sentences and in longer text—but could also provide some insight into cognitive operations of the reader during the reading act.

The major *reading comprehension paradigm* of the 1970s was keyed in limited senses to both text and reader.

Limitations of these models, however, became clearer. First, they failed in many cases to account for nonverbal aspects of the reading act. In many ways, they were too *discourse-type specific* to suggest the richness and elegance of models needed to govern research directions as complex as reading comprehension. And, finally, they became extremely complex and cumbersome in application; enough so to discourage many researchers from using them.

Their impact was clear, however. Reading research would never be the same again for many reasons, not the least of which was that the walls of the older, traditional reading scholar's domain had been irreparably breached. Linguists, philosophers, psycholinguists, sociologists, and others had moved in. Also, the most obtrusive of the new reading comprehension theory and research types —the developmental psychologists—now led the development of the latest research paradigm for reading. This represented a significant change, since behaviorist models had to be set aside.

The impact of behaviorist psychology on reading research had been significant. This particular learning theory had served as a strong assumptive base for reading research and, more importantly, for the development of theoretical models of reading, which serve as the generating sources for research design. It shaped the character of reading for decades. That is, not just research, but theoretical conceptions of what reading was and how best it should be taught were derived from the behaviorist perspective.

---

*The directions of research discused here are still being pursued by many researchers, so this discussion should not suggest that these models are no longer serving fruitful roles for reading research or theory development.

The movement to developmental psychology and a developmental approach to learning generally did not happen suddenly. In fact, one can trace the movement back to the later 1950s when Noam Chomsky wrote a detailed, blistering review of noted behaviorist B. F. Skinner's work on language (Chomsky, 1959). Chomsky's theories of language reshaped both theory and research in language acquisition and development and, subsequently, reading theory and research. The later 1960s and early 1970s abound with doctoral dissertations exploring the role of *deep structure* and other transformational grammar notions in reading comprehension, all of which derived from Chomsky's work.

About the same time, educators in this country were beginning to examine the work of Jean Piaget, the developmental psychologist, well-known throughout the rest of the world but little known here. And somewhat later the work of the Russian psychologist Lev Vygotsky and students of his, such as Alexander Luria, became accessible.

Their posture on how learning and knowing generally occurred came at a time propitious for change in reading. A scattering of studies appeared through the 1970s reflecting the impact of Piaget and his counterparts. However, their initial thrust, though counter to the behaviorist orientations, tended not to reveal, at least overtly, Piaget's impact. Gradually, though, interest in the *nontext* factors which shaped reading comprehension represented a significant departure from behaviorism as a defining psychology of learning. Developmental psychologists explored the less observable and more abstruse ideas central to comprehension. Words such as *consciousness, mind, cognitive processing,* and others began to appear in the reading literature.

By the later 1970s additional changes could be seen, as reading comprehension research turned increasingly toward the reader and away from what was being read. In addition, new language used by reading scholars reflected the impact of Piaget and other developmentalists such as Vygotsky. For example, *schema, assimilation,* and *accommodation* are key Piagetian concepts which moved into reading comprehension research in substantive fashion. Although their use is now specialized for reading, their roots are in more general learning theory and the epistemological drives of earlier developmental psychology.

Piaget had discovered that learning develops through stages, each stage having a generalized set of cognitive characteristics that determines how and what kind of learning can take place. Of critical importance to his theories is the concept of *schema*. One's schemata are essentially the mental maps of the various features and constructs of reality that he or she possesses. Learning takes place for the individual not simply by accruing more details or facts and piling them up in the mind, but rather by fitting new information into one's schema, i.e., assimilating it into the schema. Or, if the new information is dramatically new or different, one then adjusts the schema so that it is essentially altered both in general contour and in detail; i.e., one accommodates the new learning.

Consider that you do not know how to play the game of checkers. You sit at a board with a person who is going to teach you the game. When you move sideways to capture, your mentor points out that such a move is not allowed; you must jump only forward. You accept this and instruction continues. Suppose, on the other hand, that your teacher instead grabs the corners of the board, flips all of the pieces into the air, and says, "I win." You would be dumbfounded, for, although you do not know how to play the specific game of checkers, you are familiar with board games as a group and know that there are certain general rules with which they all comply. You have a schema of board games. With time and effort, you will refine your schema so that checkers becomes an increasingly detailed part of it. Your level of performance at checkers will probably plateau relatively early since it is not that important in your life. However, if you were a professional at checkers, things would be different. Hence, there are articles and books on the technicalities and strategies of checkers which most of us would have difficulty comprehending, not because we are poor readers, but because our prior experience is more limited than that of experts, and our schema of checkers is not as rich or sophisticated as is theirs. As personal experience tells us, our comprehension is affected by interest, background, and knowledge about a given subject or topic.

In some instances, our schema is so crude with respect to a given subject or idea that we cannot fit the subject into the schema, or assimilate it, as we were able to do with the game of checkers. Instead, we must alter our schema, sometimes dramatically. Consider, for example, that for some reason we had no experience with board games of any kind when the checkers incident took place—the board being flipped into the air. If that were the case, and, further, suppose that we knew only of hide-and-seek as a game, then perhaps flipping the board into the air would not seem so strange. It would deter the opponent at least. Our schema of games would have to be adjusted to fit the new information. Our schema must accommodate the new realities rather than effect an assimilation of the realities into it.

With such a conceptual framework describing learning in general, reading scholars took what seemed a natural step to make certain changes in Piaget's notions and explore their potential in researching reading comprehension. The yield has been rich, especially in establishing the critical importance of *prior knowledge* and experience—background knowledge, if you will—in reading comprehension and also in pointing out techniques and strategies for building background knowledge and in activating prior experience.

Certainly, by the beginning of the 1980s the focus of reading comprehension research had shifted to a *text-processing paradigm* and away from a *text-centered* one. The natural compromise of this research direction with earlier directions centers on the interaction between text and reader. Indeed, that appears the current direction, with the possible added dimension of context—social and otherwise—as a factor.

The past two or three decades of reading comprehension research reflect a limited but important number of general characteristics. Perhaps the most conspicuous of these is the fact that reading comprehension, as a critical part of reading, has had relatively little concentrated attention. A second thing that strikes a reviewer of the period is that once it began to receive sustained attention, the focus in reading comprehension research was determined more by circumstance of time and interest than by need or the possible practical application of such research. Until the later 1970s, reading comprehension was the stepchild of all other elements, skills, and content-drives of reading.

Third, reading comprehension has been defined over the years, not so much by any logical or psychological imperative, but rather by the convenience or state of the art of allied fields. That is, the state of knowledge in learning theory, literary theory, or linguistics has served as the driving force of theory and research pursuits in reading comprehension more than have essential questions generated within the traditional reading education field itself.

Be that as it may, reading comprehension has come into its own as a legitimate domain of study and as a critical area of instruction. Excitement lies in its youth and vigor. Challenge for the teacher rests in finding the best of what we know and using it in the most effective means possible to improve our approaches to reading comprehension instruction.

WHAT READING COMPREHENSION IS

One of the difficulties in the development of reasonable approaches to the research and teaching of reading comprehension rests in our inability, over the years, to agree on what the term *reading comprehension* means. There has not been a lack of definition attempts, for whatever they have been worth. Perhaps the most common and accurate, if the least useful, is that "reading comprehension is a complex process." Two words which are probably most commonly used in definitions of reading comprehension, however, are *meaning* and *understanding*. If a reader *comprehends* a written text, that reader obviously must know what the text *means*, i.e., must be able to *understand* what is written. Yet, consider the following:

1. Springfield is the capital of Illinois.
2. The sun always shines in the Northwest.
3. Green ideas sleep furiously.
4. Sniggles gorfle glinks.
5. What if a much of a which of a wind.

Equally proficient readers would likely disagree on the meaningfulness of many of these. Most would agree that number one is meaningful. A few would probably assert that number two is not meaningful since it is not true. (One would assume, however, that ability to assess the truth or falsity of an assertion presupposes an understanding or comprehension of the assertion.) Number three seems to be grammatically meaningful, but one does not normally think of ideas having color, nor is the adverb *furiously* associated with sleeping. Therefore, many would suggest it is not meaningful. Number four sounds like it could be meaningful, yet the words are obviously nonsense. And, finally, number five is meaningful for the poet e. e. cummings but probably not for most of us outside of some poetic or language-play context.

Historically, one of the difficulties of defining reading comprehension is reflected in the use of terms such as *meaning* or *understanding*, which suggest ambiguous interpretations, to say the least. Further, the definitions are descriptive without suggesting what processses are involved. In 1917 Thorndike defined reading comprehension as,

> a very complex procedure involving a weighing of each of many elements in a sentence, their organization in the proper relations to one another, the selection of certain of their connotations and the rejection of others, and the cooperation of many forces to produce the final response.

His definition is typical of the many offered over the years. By the 1970s there was an increasing move toward definitions which were operational in nature. That is, scholars seemed to become disenchanted with efforts at straight conceptual description and instead focused on the observable characteristics or behaviors of a reader who was an acknowledged comprehender. For example, one who comprehends what is read is one who can demonstrate the ability to infer conclusions, detect specious logic in a text, identify cause-effect relationships, and so on.

One of the advantages of such definitions is that, to a limited extent, they enable one to bypass the more demanding questions about what goes on in the reader during the act of comprehension and go directly to hierarchies of skills or subskills associated with reading performance. These skills have been and continue to be the guiding frameworks for the scope and sequence of basal reading programs and locally developed reading curricula.

The unfortunate thing about such skill lists is that they do not possess much explanatory power, although they might indicate fairly accurately the expected performance of a proficient reader. That is, knowing that good readers can infer proper conclusions in text or can detect specious reasoning does not tell us how that reader came to that conclusion or what mental processes were involved in detecting the specious reasoning, much less suggest what the most effective means are for teaching those processes or skills. In fact, examination of research into skill identification and structuring of skill hierarchy for instructional purposes fails to yield substantial evidence of support for any major skill group or skill hierarchy (Rosenshine, 1980).

Further, even if one assumed a concurrence on a general listing of skills involved in reading comprehension, what stands as acceptable performance is another issue. For example, most of us would probably agree that the level of comprehension necessary can vary from text to text and from purpose to purpose. Some information in print, ranging from an obscure article in the newspaper read for relaxation to a recipe for bread pudding read out of curiosity (even though you do not really like bread pudding and have no desire to ever make it), is information you feel no need to retain for a long period or to integrate into your conceptions of reality in a major fashion. Your reading of such material is largely superficial. While your comprehension can remain at the surface, you are not the worse for wear because of your limited involvement. However, much of what we read should be comprehended at such a level that we possess it or have a sense of ownership of it. We integrate it into our conceptions of the world to make it a fundamental part of us.

Deciding, then, on the level of performance we as teachers should expect from our students in any given reading activity becomes a difficult decision. One context and reading purpose might be a powerful one for some readers and irrelevant for others. If nothing else, this sparks renewed concern for individualizing our reading instruction.

An examination of some of the definitions of reading comprehension also reveals the differences in the interests and intents of the definer. For reading psychologists and reading theoreticians, elegant definitions of reading comprehension are those which offer potentially powerful research hypotheses about the reading process. For the classroom teacher, such elegant definitions are likely to be secondary to those which are more directly and immediately tied to instruction in reading. A teacher is primarily interested in the mental processes involved in reading where such knowledge overlaps with the logical ordering of instructional elements in the teaching of reading.

Many recent definitions of reading comprehension attempt to get at the mental processes involved in the reading act. As noted earlier, for contemporary scholars the reader is currently of more theoretical interest than is the text. However, the act of reading is a "cognitive activity embedded in social and linguistic contexts" (Bloome and Green, 1984).

As we increasingly recognize the importance of a variety of factors involved in comprehension, more contemporary definitions include reference to properties of the text, the cognitive and linguistic processes of the reader, and the features of the contexts and purposes of the reading.

It seems clear that the profession will not likely ever reach consensus on a universal definition of reading comprehension that will satisfy the needs of all reading educators, nor should there necessarily be such a definition. For our purposes, **reading comprehension is the act of using the knowledge and skills one possesses to process the information presented in the text.**

For the classroom teacher, instruction in reading comprehension is that which most directly assists the learner in:

1. Developing critical skills necessary for bringing what he or she knows to the reading act
2. Developing critical skills necessary for processing the structures and meanings of language used in text
3. Refining the mental processing capacities used in the reading act

$\times$ Therefore, legitimate and important activities in reading comprehension instruction include development of reasoning and thinking skills, development of knowledge of written language structures and forms, development of background knowledge and its application to processing of text, and development of facility in monitoring one's own reading, both objectively and critically. That is what most of the remainder of this book is about.

WHAT WE KNOW ABOUT READING COMPREHENSION

Research in reading comprehension has been particularly rich in both quantity and quality during the past ten to fifteen years, although the most impressive work has been done within the decade or so since the early 1970s. During this period there has been serious exploration of a number of areas of reading comprehension. Focus has been on text, on reader, on interaction of the two, on instructional approaches, and upon a number of combinations of these variables. Although a great deal remains to be considered, certainly inroads have been made and important questions have been answered.

To provide the most helpful way to focus a research examination for the classroom teacher of reading, the author has identified topics or categories of most concern. Six categories of research with implications for the classroom teacher are included. They are: (1) questioning; (2) picture adjuncts; (3) advance organizers; (4) text structures; (5) vocabulary; and (6) reading/writing relationships.

Questioning

Although much of the contemporary focus in reading theory and research is on the reading process, the bulk of our instructional focus continues to be upon questioning; questioning before, during, and especially after the reading. Durkin and co-workers spent almost 18,000 minutes observing reading lessons in intemediate-grade-level classrooms (Durkin, 1978-79; Guszak, 1967). Among her conclusions was the observation that teachers devote much of their instructional time to asking questions after the reading has been completed. She further noted that the questions tended to be low level (on any taxonomy of thinking levels) and literally oriented in character. Commonly they were questions students could answer with one word or a very short phrase. Reviews of basal reading programs revealed similar findings (Durkin, 1981). Perhaps even more distressing were findings that in some basal reading programs there appeared to be no coherent questioning strategies (Beck et al., 1979). The questions were often simply arrived at in a random fashion; questioning designed to lead the student in an inferential direction, or even any direction, was lacking.

During the 1960s and even into the 1970s, questioning research focused upon levels of thinking. A variety of taxonomies appeared—the Bloom taxononomy, the Barrett taxonomy, the Sanders taxonomy, and others. They were important since they drew our attention to the recognition of different levels of thinking required by different questions.

We practiced categorizing questions and writing questions to fit the various taxonomic levels. Unfortunately, we also developed a sort of tacit belief that plying the taxonomic range with our questions was enough to assure both comprehension of the text and the development of thinking skills in the learner. Research since indicates that questioning strategies may be even more fundamental to text comprehension than is simply exposing the learner to a variety of levels of questions (Hansen and Pearson, 1980; Hansen and Pearson, 1983). The placement of the question, its content, its semantic character, and its relationship to the learners' prior experience are all important factors in designing a questioning strategy.

Prior Experience

A commonly espoused generalization about reading comprehension is, "The more you know about the subject at hand to be read, the more you take away from the reading." Common sense tells us that a doctor should be able to comprehend an article in a medical journal more readily than can a lay person.

Further, one's prior knowledge also determines the kind of information gained from the reading. During the 1970s, considerable research established this fact. Typical was the work done by Anderson and others (Anderson and Pichert, 1978; Anderson et al., 1977). Anderson presented contrived text to different audiences with different backgrounds and interests. In one case, the text—which could be interpreted as either a musical performance or a wrestling match (not an easy text to contrive!)—was presented to two different undergraduate college student audiences, a group of music majors and a group of physical education majors. As one would suspect, each group interpreted the text to fit their prior knowledge and interest.

Another study, by Bransford and McCarrell (1974), used a line which has become a near classic for demonstrating the importance of prior knowledge. "The notes were sour because the seams were split" makes sense *if* you are familiar with bagpipes but not necessarily otherwise.

The Anderson and Bransford research illustrates not only the importance of prior experience and knowledge from an information-base point of view but also the closely interrelated role of schema elaboration in determining effective comprehension. One's schema of "bagpipes" is critical to the quality of comprehension that takes place. Schema and knowledge base are both important. Schemata are shaped by information; information is shaped by schemata.

Interaction of text and reader was demonstrated in a number of studies during the 1970s (Anderson et al., 1979; Bransford and Johnson, 1972; Kail et al., 1977; and others).

Since that time, much of the instructionally oriented research on means to exploit prior knowledge and enhance schemata has centered on the role and use of questioning. And, although there are opportunities for the teacher to activate or build background knowledge during and after the reading, both research and teaching have concentrated on the prereading phase of instruction. During the prereading phase, the options open to the teacher are essentially two. The teacher can provide necessary experiences relevant to the subject matter to be taught; or the teacher can establish analogous associations so that students can make important connections between what they already know and what is to be read that they probably do not know.

Research in kinds of questions during the prereading phase suggests that these have much to do with the quality of comprehension. Recent research, for example, suggests that higher-level inferential questions asked both during and after selection reading enhance *both* comprehension of the selection at hand and comprehension of new selections (Hansen 1981; Hansen and Pearson 1983; Graves & Cooke, 1980; Graves et al., 1983; Hayes and Tierney, 1982).

Analogies

Among the most interesting of the prereading questioning strategies are those which are premised upon analogical ties. Using analogies, of course, means using an idea or a construct that bears important similarities to the ideas or information in the text. Indeed, the logic of the analogy is powerful. It allows the teacher to take what the student knows and use that as a basic comparison to establish critical areas of similarity. Over the years both philosophers and psychologists have argued for its instructional value. However, research results have been somewhat mixed regarding its value as a tool in teaching reading comprehension. Some studies examining the potential of analogies in comprehending problem-solving text indicate the analogy must fit tightly (Perfetti et al., 1983). Some studies found no role for use of analogy (Drugge, 1977; and others). Other, recent studies suggest that there is potential for analogy strategies to improve comprehension (Hayes and Matya, 1981; Hayes and Tierney, 1982).

Unfortunately, most research on analogy application concentrates on the nature of the analogy itself: its tightness-of-fit, its semantic complexity, or its use in nontext-direct comprehension contexts. Not enough attention has been given to strategies of questioning which can be structured by the analogy itself.

Consideration of the power of analogical strategy to activate prior knowledge during the prereading has more than a logical appeal to it. Research on questioning strategies that use higher-level inferential questions to predict outcomes in text based upon use of prior knowledge has suggested that reading comprehension can be significantly improved as a result (Hansen and Hubbard, 1984). Through inferential questioning students are encouraged to predict what might take place in the story to be read. If the teacher can establish or assist in establishing analogies to attach the predictions to, the opportunities for inferring more logical options increase.

Postreading Questions

Experimental data on the value of postreading questions are mixed. Nungester and Duchastel (1982) found that postreading questions were more effective than text review. Related research on the potential of this type of questioning lends support to Nungester and Duchastel (Ellis et al., 1982). However, other researchers have found postreading questions not effective or even restrictive in some cases (Wixson, 1981; Sagaria and DiVesta, 1978; and others). It must be remembered that some researchers exploring the role of prereading questioning suggest using follow-up questions that tie the reading to earlier predictions made by the reader. There appears to be increasing support for designing questioning strategies that use questions throughout the entire instructional sequence, from prereading to postreading activities.

Student Questions

Within the past decade, interest in the potential of metacognitive activities and techniques for improving reading comprehension has increased significantly. We know that better readers are good *self-monitors*. They approach reading tasks with an understanding of how effective reading takes place. They know how to infer the main idea. They know how to keep important questions in mind as they read. In brief, they "know how to know." Metalanguage is language about language. Metacognition is knowing how you know. Metalinguistic and metacognitive capacities develop, but can they or should they be taught directly?

One advocated approach is that of teaching students to be *self-questioners*, i.e., to question themselves during the reading. Some studies have found the strategy to be ineffective (Duell, 1974; Morse, 1976; and others). Others, however, have responded more positively (Andre and Anderson, 1978-79; Meichenbaum and Asarnow, 1978; and others). Tierney and Cunningham (1984) have been critical of many of the former studies for ignoring important aspects of questioning strategies being taught to students, especially in those studies with results of no significant difference.

Many of the metacognitive strategies designed to improve comprehension contain additional elements beyond student self-questioning. Therefore, it is difficult to determine the impact of questioning as a variable interacting with other, often more prominent, variables. Several studies, however, have yielded positive results involving these strategies. For example, Brown provided frameworks for second-grade through seventh-grade students to assist in comprehension of text read to them. The framework enhanced recall and comprehension (Brown et al., 1977).

In a major study, where cognitive development and enhancement was emphasized, Kathryn Au reported the results of a cognitive training program used to teach reading comprehension to first through third graders in Hawaii. In the program, the teacher's questions encouraged children to express ideas, tie events to stories, and make inferences from the text. Reading performance improved substantially (Au, 1977; Au and Kawakami, in press).

Examination of this body of research and the reviews of other related research suggests a consensus of support for instruction in the use of metacognitive strategies.

Picture Adjuncts

Do pictures help students comprehend text? Some studies concluded that pictures play no significant role in assisting comprehension of text (Marr, 1977; Samuels, 1970; Thomas, 1979). However, other studies have found facilitative effects in pictures (Ruch and Levin, 1977; and others). They found that pictures have a greater effect when they are related to key ideas or concepts in the text and when their use is part of a larger comprehension strategy being applied in the reading or in the reading instruction. Their potential for use in a strategy to activate prior knowledge as well as their prospective role as part of an advance organizer approach are obvious.

The role of pictures appears fairly solid in most major basal reading programs. Of course, they have always been instrumental to the sale and use of tradebook literature. Given that they are well entrenched, it appears reasonable to exploit their potential as effectively as possible.

Advance Organizers

Determining effectiveness of *advance organizers* presents some difficulty since there appears not to be wide agreement on what an advance organizer is. Assuming, however, the broadest possible definition—that is, one that includes previews, outlines, text framing, study guides, and other introductory guideline questions, as well as many of the contemporary text-monitoring strategies advocated as metacognitive or metacomprehension approaches—we can see useful results.

One advocated strategy is that of *inducing imagery*; the image can be derived from a metaphor or key analogy established in the text, or it can be an image of a key character in a story. Its source seems less important than its image-inducing potential. As a guide to the reading of the text, image inducing can be viewed as an advance organizer of sorts, although its use during the reading and after are also obvious. The research indicates that such strategies seem to work most effectively with older students (above the fourth grade) and with shorter passages or texts. Longer text presents greater difficulty for a single or limited image that serves key roles (Levin, 1973; Levin and Wolff, 1972; Linden and Wittrock, 1981; and others). Younger children have difficulty sustaining the image over the duration of the reading. Even in older students, many learners appear to be verbal rather than visual or image-oriented.

Still, it seems reasonable to conclude that as an approach to instruction and in an advance organizer role especially, image-inducing strategies have gathered a strong base of research and practice support. In particular, their appeal in teaching certain types of nonfiction, e.g., poetry, seems obvious.

Although summarizing is normally done after the reading of a text, a number of studies have examined the usefulness of the practice when instruction or an outline is presented prior to the reading, as an advance organizer. These studies have found the practice to be effective, especially with older students (Brown et al., 1981; and others).

Studies in metacomprehension can also fall into the advance organizer category when the learner is presented with guides prior to the reading. Palincsar (1982), for example, found reciprocal teaching strategies effective ways to improve comprehension. Notetaking was also found to be an effective means for helping readers generate inferences and elaborate text (Peper and Mayer, 1978).

Perhaps one of the more popular advance organizer strategies is that incorporating the study guide. Study guides are components of basal reading programs or teacher-designed programs and usually consist of guide questions designed to structure the reading of the assigned text. Although there is not an extensive research base in the use of study guides, what we do have suggests that they can be helpful for some kinds of texts and for some students (Anthony, 1981; and others).

Given the theoretical and practical support for the importance of internal monitoring skills in the effective reader, it only makes sense to work toward the development and implementation of a diversity of techniques and stragegies that are designed to help the developing reader acquire such skills. Good study skill development, including effective use of study guides, appears a natural part of this effort.

Text Structures

Although contemporary research seems more interested in the reader than in the text, most authorities would still concur that text, its forms and structures, represents an important aspect of reading and of reading instruction.

There remains a legitimate conviction that interaction of reader and text can occur effectively only when the reader knows enough about language structure generally and its specifics in text in particular to effect the interaction. Even if meaning resides in the reader, its evocation requires knowledge of language and text structure.

Story Grammar

From a research and practice standpoint, story grammar or story structure is one of the more controversial areas of text structure. The issue is not so much whether there is such a structure or grammar, for it is accepted that there is. Nor is there an issue over which grammar is best, for there are a number of story grammars just as there are a variety of sentence structure grammars; they all have certain advantages and certain disadvantages. The story grammar one prefers depends upon the use or uses to be made of the grammar.

All story grammars include certain basic elements such as setting, plot, character development, protagonist/antagonist relationships, problem, problem resolution, climax, and so on. They vary primarily in their complexity and sophistication. Further, most reading authorities agree that *sense of story*, or an implicit understanding of the elements and their sequence in story grammars, is important to the comprehension of stories.

The primary issue appears to be whether or not direct instruction in story grammar and its use or whether questioning strategies designed strictly around the elements of structure in a story grammar are helpful or desirable as part of the reading program. There has been substantial research to suggest that such instruction does produce more effective comprehension. Bowman (1981) found that questioning strategies based on story structure had positive results with sixth graders, and a variety of other studies have found evidence supporting the idea of using a story map or structure to guide questioning strategies (Beck, 1984; Gordon and Pearson, 1983; Singer and Donlan, 1982; and others).

There is some evidence to suggest that individuals who possess a sense of story structure benefit less from such strategies than do those less experienced with literature.

Nonfiction Structures

Just as fiction text possesses structure in the form of story grammar, nonfiction text reflects structure in the form of narration and exposition. Most research has been on exposition, where a variety of structural models have been proposed (Meyer, 1975; and others). Instructional approaches to expository text structure usually include activities requiring students to diagram or outline content relationships in the text. Ideas are diagrammed or presented schematically and are then used as a study guide of sorts. Some researchers found that this method helped with reading the assigned text at hand, as well as providing some transfer effect (Bartlett, 1978; Mosenthal, 1983). Others appear to be more skeptical, perhaps often because the network or mapping models are so complex. This might be an area where the jury is still out.

Vocabulary

Although we undoubtedly have much yet to learn about the role of vocabularly in reading, it still represents one area where research has been substantial over the years. Correlational and factor-analytic studies over the years consistently have revealed high correlations between vocabulary and reading ability. We know that vocabulary is one of the most accurate and useful predictors of reading ability. Why then the continued focus on vocabulary-oriented research? One reason is that there still remains considerable disagreement on exactly what the role of vocabularly is in reading. Another concerns how vocabulary should be taught, i.e., directly or as part of a schema-oriented approach to reading instruction. Some, such as Becker (1977), propose direct vocabulary-building instruction. Others suggest that knowledge acquisition generally and a schema-oriented approach are needed where linguistic and experiential contexts are instrumental (Goodman, 1976; Johnson and Pearson, 1978; and others).

There would appear to be both theoretical and practical support for a best-of-both-worlds position. Recent studies such as that by Adams and Huggins (1985) support the need for direct vocabulary instruction for improving students' acquisition of critical sight words and beyond. Yet the wide body of research correlating vocabulary knowledge and verbal abilities, and reasoning abilities and reading comprehension generally, suggest the importance of a reading program designed to immerse students in a range of quality literature and provide them with a rich oral language environment (Michael et al., 1951; Terman, 1918; and others).

Word Identification

In their recent review of word identification research, Johnson and Baumann (1984) infer a number of generalizations with instructional implications that appear to support the best-of-both-worlds need. From the standpoint of phonics instruction, they suggest that the research indicates that "programs emphasizing early, reasonably intensive phonics instruction produce readers who are more proficient at word pronunciation than programs emphasizing meaning." They also suggest that direct instruction in sequence of analysis-segmentation-blending is most successful, and that some evidence suggests that visual pattern-recognition training in letter components facilitates word identification for beginning readers. Yet they also point out that direct instruction in word identification did not necessarily carry over to improved comprehension. Other research in the instruction of preselection vocabulary suggests the importance of a meaningful context, appropriate use of prior experience, and selection of vocabulary that bears key conceptual ties to important ideas in the text (Beck et al., 1982; Stevens, 1982; and others).

These data suggest that instructional strategies in word attack—even when established as effective in the teaching of decoding skills—probably has limited carryover into vocabulary acquisition and utilization as part of reading comprehension. Again, this would appear to support a comprehensive approach to reading vocabulary instruction.

Perhaps the ultimate irony in the quagmire of reading vocabulary research is that after all the years of work, we are still using relatively crude means of measuring vocabulary knowledge and growth. This appears enough of a problem for Anderson and Freebody (1979) to suggest that our first step ought to be the development of improved methods of assessing breadth of vocabulary knowledge.

Unfortunately, instruction cannot wait for this sort of refinement in research methodology.

Reading/Writing Relationships

One of the major contemporary interests in reading comprehension lies in the relationship between reading and writing. It seems a logical extension in the search for an increasing number of variables outside the text itself. And, since the writing process according to some bears a striking resemblance to the reading process, writing seems a good direction to pursue.

It is probably safe to assert that over the years research on the reading/writing relationship has not been extensive; the majority of what has been done is correlational in nature. Perhaps the most extensive correlational work was done by Walter Loban (1963), who followed a group of students from kindergarten through high school and tracked their development in all the language-consuming and language-producing skill areas of the language arts. He found high correlation between reading performance and writing performance and found that the relationship became more pronounced as one got into the upper grades. Loban's work is probably the best known in this area of research, but it has plenty of company. Schonell (1942), Fishco (1966), Woodfin (1968), and Grimmer (1970) are but a few of the studies correlating reading and writing performance. These works focused on a number of variables, while other correlational studies examined specific variables. For example, work by Heil (1970), Perron (1977), Combs (1979), and others found positive correlation between the syntactic- or grammar-producing abilities of learners at various grade levels and their reading ability. Although there have been some studies finding little or no correlation in this area, they still represent a minority of the total correlational studies (Siedow, 1973; and others).

Experimental studies that have incorporated writing into the instruction of reading comprehension have had some success. Doctorow et al. (1978) found that grade six students who wrote one-sentence summaries for paragraph headings after each paragraph they read in a story had greater comprehension and recall than those in either control or placebo settings. Other similar studies that incorporated writing into reading instruction have found similar success (Kulhavy et al., 1975).

Unfortunately, the overall research suggests that the impact of reading on writing development is very little. The transfer effect appears to be primarily in the opposite direction, i.e., from writing to reading. Further, the most impressive results in the use of writing to assist reading comprehension come when **the writing is built into the reading instruction,** rather than used solely as a supplement to the reading instruction.

Given the instructional direction suggested by research, it is somewhat discouraging to examine current reading curricula, both locally developed and in the form of basal reading programs. Writing activities appear largely as supplements to the instruction rather than integral to it. Students write prior to the reading, or are asked to write reports or stories as part of the *Follow-up Activities* or *Lesson Extension Activities* or *Lesson Enrichment Activities;* the name varies, but the concept does not. The writing is used to supplement the direct instruction in reading and is not an integral part of that instruction.

Research in reading/writing relationships points out some fruitful avenues of pursuit. It is up to the profession to capitalize upon them and invoke the necessary changes in reading instruction.

HIGHLIGHTS

Although there has been an historic interest in reading comprehension, its role as a critical part of a reading program is a relatively recent development.

There is no one definition of reading comprehension that is accepted by all authorities and practitioners in reading education. One's definition of reading comprehension is determined by the purpose of the application.

Focus on reading comprehension theory and research over the past two decades has moved from a primary concern for the complexity of the text to the processing of the text by the reader. Some call this difference a *text-driven* approach versus a *reader-driven* approach. Although it is an over-simplification to separate the two, the terms *bottom-driven* and *bottom-up* are used to represent the view that the structure and semantics of the language in text shape the meaning conveyed. *Top-down* refers to the view that meaning is conceptualized by the reader and imposed upon the text.

The contemporary approach is best viewed as one that recognizes the interaction of the reader and the text in determining meaning.

Research in reading comprehension over the past several years has reflected the theoretical interests of the time. That is, much of the work in the latter 1960s and first half of the 1970s focused largely on comprehension of text where structure, semantics, or propositional content were viewed as variables.

By the latter 1970s and into the 1980s interest in the reader's mental processing was predominant, with contemporary concerns on the interactions of reader and text. Important findings of that research are:

1. Prior experience (background knowledge) is a critical factor in determining comprehension of a text. The more one knows about the subject to be read, the more one takes away from the reading.
2. One's schemata play important roles in comprehending text.
3. One's conception of the context and purpose of the reading plays an important role in comprehending text.
4. Knowing the structure of expository text, narrative text, and grammars of stories helps in the comprehension of those texts.
5. Vocabulary development occurs as a function of both direct instruction and indirect instruction concerned with establishing a rich, meaning-based learning context.
6. Writing can help reading comprehension when it is used as an ongoing, integral part of the instruction as well as a supplement to it.

ADDITIONAL SELECTED READINGS

An Idea Whose Time Has Come

DEVINE, T. (1986). *Teaching reading comprehension: From theory to practice.* Boston: Allyn and Bacon.

FLOOD, J. (Ed.) (1984). *Promoting reading comprehension.* Newark, Del.: IRA.

FLOOD, J. (Ed.) (1984). *Understanding reading comprehension.* Newark, Del.: IRA.

IRWIN, J. (1986). *Teaching reading comprehension processes.* Englewood Cliffs, N.J.: Prentice Hall.

MCNEIL, J. (1984). *Reading comprehension.* Glenview, Ill.: Scott, Foresman and Co.

PEARSON, P. D. and JOHNSON, D. (1978). *Teaching reading comprehension.* New York: Holt, Rinehart and Winston.

What Reading Comprehension Is

DURKIN, D. (Jan. 1981). What is the value of the new interest in reading comprehension? *Language Arts*, 23-43.

KINTSCH, W. (1974). *The representation of meaning in memory.* Hillsdale, N.J.: Erlbaum Assoc.

LABERGE, D. and SAMUELS, S. J. (Eds.) (1977). *Basic processes in reading: Perception and comprehension.* Hillsdale, N.J.: Erlbaum Assoc.

What We Know About Reading Comprehension

PEARSON, P. D. (Ed.) (1984). *Handbook of reading research.* New York: Longman.

Note also technical reports from the Center for the Study of Reading, University of Illinois–Urbana, Urbana, Illinois.

REFERENCES

ADAMS, M. J. AND HUGGINS, A.W.F. (1985). *The growth of children's sight vocabulary: A quick test with educational and theoretical implications* (Technical Report no. 330). Urbana, Ill.: Center for the Study of Reading, University of Illinois.

ANDERSON, R. C. AND FREEBODY, P. (1979). *Vocabulary knowledge and reading* (Technical Report no. 11). Urbana, Ill.: Center for the Study of Reading, University of Illinois.

ANDERSON, R. C. AND PICHERT, J. W. (1978). Recall of previously unrecallable information following a shift in perspective. *Journal of Verbal Learning and Verbal Behavior, 17,* 1-12.

ANDERSON, R. C., PICHERT, J. W. AND SHIREY, L. L. (1979). *Effects of the reader's schema at different points in time* (Technical Report no. 119). Urbana, Ill.: Center for the Study of Reading, University of Illinois.

ANDERSON, R. C., REYNOLDS, R. E., SCHALLERT, D. C. AND GOETZ, E. T. (1977). Frameworks for comprehending discourse. *American Education Journal, 14,* 357-382.

ANDRE, M. AND ANDERSON, T. H. (1978-1979). The development and evaluation of a self-questioning study technique. *Reading Research Quarterly, 14,* 605-623.

ANTHONY, P. E. (1981). An evaluation of an inductive method for teaching three skills necessary for reading narrative fiction. Unpublished doctoral dissertation, Boston University.

AU, K. (Dec. 1977). Cognitive training and reading achievement. Paper presented at meeting of the Association for the Advancement of Behavior Therapy, Atlanta, Ga.

AU, K. AND KAWAKAMI, A. (in press). The influence of the social organization of instruction on children's text comprehension ability: A Vygotskian perspective. In T. E. Raphael and R. Reynolds (Eds.), *Contexts of school-based literacy.* New York: Longman.

BARTLETT, B. J. (1978). Top-level structure as an organizational strategy for recall of classroom text. Unpublished doctoral dissertation, Arizona State University.

BECK, I. L. (1984). Developing comprehension: The impact of the directed reading lesson. In R. Anderson, J. Osborn, and R. Tierney (Eds.), *Learning to read in American schools: Basal readers and content texts.* Hillsdale, N.J.: Erlbaum Assoc.

BECK, I. L., MCKEOWN, M., MCCASLIN, E. AND BURKES, A. (1979). *Instructional dimensions that may effect reading comprehension: Examples from two commercial reading programs.* Pittsburgh, Pa.: University of Pittsburgh, Learning Research and Development Center.

BECK, I. L., PERFETTI, C. AND MCKEOWN, M. G. (1982). Effects of long-term vocabulary instruction on lexical access and reading comprehension. *Journal of Educational Psychology, 74,* 506-521.

BECKER, W. C. (1977). Teaching reading and language to the disadvantaged—What we have learned from field research. *Harvard Educational Review, 47,* 518-543.

BLOOME, D. AND GREEN, J. (1984). Directons in the sociolinguistic study of reading. In P. D. Pearson et al., *Handbook of reading research.* New York: Longman.

BOND, G. AND DYKSTRA, R. (1967). The cooperative research program in first grade reading instruction. *Reading Research Quarterly, 2,* 1-142.

BOWMAN, M. A. (1981). The effect of story structure questioning upon the comprehension and metacognitive awareness of sixth grade students. Unpublished doctoral dissertation, University of Maryland.

BRANSFORD, J. AND JOHNSON, M. (1972). Contextual prerequisites for understanding. Some investigations of comprehension and recall. *Journal of Verbal Learning and Verbal Behavior, 11,* 717-726.

BRANSFORD, J. D. AND McCARRELL, N. S. (1974). A sketch of a cognitive approach to comprehension. In W. B. Weiner and D. Palmero (Eds.), *Cognition and the symbolic process.* Hillsdale, N.J.: Erlbaum Assoc.

BROWN, A. L., CAMPIONE, J. C. AND DAY, J. D. (1981). Learning to learn: On training students to learn from texts. *Educational Researcher, 10,* 14-21.

BROWN, A. L. ET AL. (1977). Intrusion of a thematic idea in children's comprehension and retention of stories. *Child Development, 48,* 1454-1466.

CHALL, J. (1967). *Learning to read: The great debate.* New York: McGraw-Hill.

CHOMSKY, N. (1959). Review of B. F. Skinner's *Verbal Behavior. Language, 35,* 26-58.

COMBS, W. (1979). Examining the fit of practice in syntactic manipulation and scores of reading comprehension. In D. Dacker et al. (Eds.), *Sentence-combining and the teaching of writing.* Conway, Ark.: University of Central Arkansas.

DAVIS, F. B. (1944). Fundamental factors of comprehension in reading. *Psychometrika, 9,* 185-197.

DOCTOROW, M., WITTROCK, M. C. AND MARKS, C. (1978). Generative processes in reading comprehension. *Journal of Educational Psychology, 70,* 109-118.

DRUGGE, N. L. (1977). The facilitating effect of selected analogies on understanding of scientific explanations. Unpublished doctoral dissertation, University of Alberta.

DUELL, O. K. (1974). Effect of types of objective, level of test questions, and judged importance of tested materials upon posttest performance. *Journal of Educational Psychology, 66,* 225-232.

DURKIN, D. (1981). Reading instruction in five basal reading series. *Reading Research Quarterly, 16,* 515-544.

DURKIN, D. (1978-1979). What classroom observations reveal about reading comprehension instruction. *Reading Research Quarterly, 14,* 481-533.

ELLIS, J. A. ET AL. (1982). Comparative effects of adjunct postquestions and instructions on learning from text. *Journal of Educational Psychology, 74,* 860-867.

FISHCO, D. T. (1966). A study of the relationship between creativity in writing and comprehension in reading of selected seventh grade students. Unpublished doctoral dissertation, *Dissertation Abstracts International, 27.*

GOODMAN, K. S. (1976). Behind the eye: What happens in reading. In H. Singer and R. B. Ruddell (Eds.), *Theoretical models and processes of reading.* Newark, Del.: IRA.

GORDON, C. AND PEARSON, P. D. (1983). *Effects of instruction in metacomprehension abilities* (Technical Report no. 269). Urbana, Ill.: Center for the Study of Reading, University of Illinois.

GRAVES, M. F. AND COOKE, C. L. (1980). Effects of previewing difficult short stories for high school students. *Research on Reading in Secondary Schools, 6,* 38-54.

GRAVES, M. F., COOKE, C. L. AND LA BERGE, M. J. (1983). Effects of previewing difficult short stories on low ability junior high school students' comprehension, recall and attitudes. *Reading Research Quarterly, 18,* 262-276.

GRAY, W. S. AND LEARY, B. E. (1935). *What makes a book readable: An initial study.* Chicago: The University of Chicago Press.

GRIMMER, F. (1970). The effects of an experimental program in written composition on the writing of second grade children. Unpublished doctoral dissertation, University of Georgia.

GUSZAK, F. J. (1967). Teacher questioning and reading. *The Reading Teacher, 21,* 227-234.

HALLIDAY, H.A.K. AND HANSAN, R. (1976). *Cohesion in English.* London: Longman.

HANSEN, J. (1981). The effects of inference training and practice on young children's reading comprehension. *Reading Research Quarterly, 16,* 391-417.

HANSEN, J. AND HUBBARD, R. (1984). Poor readers can draw inferences. *The Reading Teacher, 37,* 586-589.

HANSEN, J. AND PEARSON, P. D. (1980). *The effects of inference training and practice on young children's comprehension* (Technical Report no. 166). Urbana, Ill.: Center for the Study of Reading, University of Illinois.

HANSEN, J. AND PEARSON, P. D. (1983). An instructional study: Improving the inferential comprehension of fourth grade good and poor readers. *Journal of Educational Psychology, 75,* 821-829.

HAYES, D. A. AND MATYA, J. A. (April, 1981). Long-term transfer effect of metaphoric allusion. Unpublished paper presented at meeting of Ameican Educational Research Association.

HAYES, D. A. AND TIERNEY, R. J. (1982). Developing readers' knowledge through analogy. *Reading Research Quarterly, 17,* 256-280.

HEIL, H. (1970). The development of an experimental program in written composition on the writing of second grade children. Unpublished doctoral dissertation, University of Georgia.

HUEY, E. B. (1908, 1968). *The psychology and pedagogy of reading.* New York: Macmillan; Republished: Cambridge, Mass.: MIT Press.

JOHNSON, D. AND BAUMANN, J. (1984). Word identification. In P. D. Pearson et al. (Eds.), *Handbook of reading research.* New York: Longman.

JOHNSON, D. AND PEARSON, P. D. (1978). *Teaching reading vocabulary.* New York: Holt, Rinehart and Winston.

KAIL JR., R. V., CHI, M. T., INGRAM, A. C. AND DANNER, F. W. Constructive aspects of children's reading comprehension. *Child Development, 48,* 684-688.

KINTSCH, W. (1974). *The representation of meaning in memory.* Hillsdale, N.J.: Erlbaum Assoc.

KINTSCH, W. AND VAN DIJK, T. (1978). Toward a model of text comprehension and production. *Psychology Review, 85,* 363-394.

KULHAVY, R., DYER, J., AND SILVER, L. (1975). The effects of notetaking and test expectancy on the learning of text material. *Journal of Educational Research, 68,* 363-365.

LEVIN, J. R. (1973). Inducing comprehension in poor readers: A test of a recent model. *Journal of Educational Psychology, 65,* 19-24.

LEVIN, J. R. AND WOLFF, P. (1972). The role of overt activity in children's imagery production. *Child Development, 43,* 537-547.

LINDEN, M. AND WITTROCK, M. C. (1981). The teaching of reading comprehension according to the model of generative learning. *Reading Research Quarterly, 17,* 44-57.

LOBAN, W. (1963). *The language of elementary school children* (Research Report no. 1). Urbana, Ill.: National Council of Teachers of English.

LORGE, I. (1939). Predicting reading difficulty of selections for children. *Elementary English Review, 16,* 229-233.

MARR, M. B. (1979). Children's comprehension of pictorial and textual event sequences. In M. L. Kamil and A. J. Moe (Eds.), *Reading research: Studies and applications.* Clemson, S. C.: National Reading Conference.

MEICHENBAUM, D. AND ASARNOW, J. (1978). Cognitive-behavior modification of metacognitive development: Implications for the classroom. In P. Kendall and S. Hollen (Eds.), *Cognitive-behavioral interventions: Theory, research and procedures.* New York: Academic Press.

MEYER, B.F.J. (1975). *The organization of prose and its effect on memory.* Amsterdam: North Holland Publishing Co.

MICHAEL, W. B., ZIMMERMAN, W. S. AND GUILFORD, J. P. (1951). An investigation of the nature the spatial relations and visualization factors in two high school samples. *Education and Psychology Measurement, 11,* 561-577.

MORSE, J. M. (1976). Effect of reader-generated questions on learning from prose. In W. D. Miller and G. H. McNich (Eds.), *Reflections and investigations on reading.* Clemson, S.C.: National Reading Conference.

MOSENTHAL, J. (1983). Instruction in the interpretation of a writer's argument: A training study. Unpublished doctoral dissertation, University of Illinois.

NUNGESTER, R. J. AND DUCHASTEL, P. C. (1982). Testing versus review: Effects on retention. *Journal of Educational Psychology, 74,* 18-22.

PALINSCAR, A. (1982). Improving the reading comprehension of junior high students through the reciprocal teaching of comprehension-monitoring activities. Unpublished doctoral dissertation, University of Illinois.

PEPER, R. J. AND MAYER, R. E. (1978). Note taking as a generative activity. *Journal of Educational Psychology, 70*, 514-522.

PERFETTI, G. A., BRANSFORD, J. D. AND FRANKS, J. J. (1983). Constraints on access in a problem-solving context. *Memory and cognition, 11*, 24-31.

PERRON, J. (1977). *The impact of mode on written syntactic complexity: Part IV-across the grades' differences and general summary* (Studies in Language Education, Report no. 30). Athens, Ga.: University of Georgia.

ROSENSHINE, B. (1980). Skill hierarchies in reading comprehension. In R. Spiro, B. Bruce, and W. Brewer (Eds.), *Theoretical issues in reading comprehension*. Hillsdale, N.J.: Erlbaum Assoc.

RICH, M. D. AND LEVIN, J. R. (1977). Pictorial organization versus verbal repetition of children's prose: Evidence for processing differences. *AV Communication Review, 25*, 269-280.

RUMELHART, D. (1977). Toward an interactive model of reading. In S. Dornic (Ed.), *Attention and performance VI*. Hillsdale, N.J.: Erlbaum Assoc.

SAGARIA, S. D. AND DiVESTA, F. J. (1978). Learner expectations induced by adjunct questions and the retrieval of intentional and incidental information. *Journal of Educational Psychology, 70*, 280-288.

SAMUELS, S. J. (1970). Effects of pictures on learning to read, comprehension and attitudes. *Review of Educational Research 40*, 397-407.

SCHONELL, F. (1942). *Backwardness in the basic subjects*. Toronto: Clarke, Irwin.

SIEDOW, M. (1973). Relationships between syntactic maturity in oral and written language and reading comprehension of materials of varying syntactic complexity. Unpublished doctoral dissertation, Indiana University.

SINGER, H. AND DONLAN, D. (1982). Active comprehension: Problem solving schema with question generation for comprehension of complex short stories. *Reading Research Quarterly, 17*, 166-186.

STEIN, N. AND GLENN, C. (1979). How children understand stories: A developmental analysis. In L. Katz (Ed.), *Current Topics in Early Childhood Education* (Vol 2).

STEVENS, K. C. (1982). Can we improve reading by teaching background information? *Journal of Reading, 25*, 326-329.

TERMAN, L. M. (1918). Vocabulary test as a measure of intelligence. *Journal of Educational Psychology, 9*, 452-466.

THOMAS, J. L. (1978) The influence of pictorial illustrations with written text and previous achievement on the reading comprehension of fourth grade science students. *Journal of Research in Science Teaching, 15*, 401-405.

THORNDIKE, E. L. (1917). Reading as reasoning: A study of mistakes in paragraph reading. *Journal of Educational Psychology, 8*, 323-332.

TIERNEY, R. J. AND CUNNINGHAM, J. W. (1984). Research of teaching reading comprehension. In P. D. Pearson (Ed.), *Handbook of reading research*. New York: Longman.

VYGOTSKY, L (1978). *Mind in Society*. Cambridge: Harvard University Press.

WIXSON, K. K. (1981). The effects of postreading questions on children's comprehension and learning. In M. L. Kamil (Ed.), *Directions in reading: Research and instruction* (30th Yearbook of the National Reading Conference). Washington, D. C.: National Reading Conference.

WOODFIN, M. (1968). Correlations among certain factors and the written expression of third grade children. *Educational and Psychological Measurement, 28*, 1237-1242.

2

Questioning

THE IMPORTANCE OF QUESTIONING

Of all the things a teacher can do or use to teach reading comprehension at any grade level, the use of questions is vitally important. Questioning is part of the ongoing spoken exchange between human beings, so it is probably the most natural approach to instruction that exists. Remember the Socratic method from ancient Greece? Remember your own learning experiences as a child growing up and as a student in school? More often than not we identify our best teachers not only with what they knew about what they taught, but also by their ability to bring out the best in us through their clever and creative questions.

With the current interest in improving classroom instruction of reading comprehension, questions and their use have received considerable attention. Throughout the 1960s and into the 1970s we devoted much energy to learning the various taxonomies of questions that had been developed and how to use them in our classes for both instructing and testing our students. Most of us were introduced to the Bloom taxonomy first, but Bloom proved to be somewhat cumbersome and overly detailed for most classroom teachers to learn and use consistently. Simpler taxonomies such as the Sanders taxonomy followed in the mid-1960s, followed by a number of others, including the Barrett—perhaps the best known to many teachers of reading.

The discussions on taxonomies taught us the importance and potential of asking questions of our students that required a range of thinking levels from them. Our earliest uses of these taxonomies were premised upon the assumption that students should be encouraged to think at all levels, from memory to synthesis and evaluation. And, if we asked a variety of questions and question types, both during instruction and on tests, and these questions plied the range of the questioning taxonomy, then our students would not only learn the content better, but they would also develop their thinking abilities more effectively.

Contemporary research in reading comprehension indicates that many of our assumptions were wrong. We know now that simply plying the range of a questioning taxonomy is not good enough. In fact, research indicates that we are probably better off not even bothering with the lower-level questions if we are aiming at higher-level comprehension, i.e., inference from implicit data (Cunningham and Tierney, 1984; Hansen and Pearson, 1983; and others).

In addition, research indicates that it is not the nature of the questions or question level alone that is important so much as it is the pattern or patterns of questions and question combinations used throughout the entire reading lesson that is important (Bowman, 1981; Ellis, 1982; and others).

Part of the difficulty with patterns, at least, is that quite often we do not make an effective distinction between a questioning activity, a questioning technique, and a questioning strategy. We often use the terms *activity, technique,* and *strategy* interchangeably, without thinking of how they are alike and how they are different. Making that distinction is an important step in the use of effective questioning to improve the instruction of reading comprehension.

STRATEGIES, TECHNIQUES, AND ACTIVITIES

Perhaps the best way to think of the three terms—*activity, technique,* and *strategy*—is as an inverted triangle divided into three layers with strategy at the top, technique in the middle, and activity at the bottom, for example:

A strategy is a global or overall plan for teaching a lesson or unit; it is an approach that incorporates techniques and activities. Normally, a questioning strategy encompasses all three phases of the reading lesson—prereading, reading, and postreading—although it could focus upon only one of these phases. The strategy assures that questions asked in all phases of the reading lesson are designed to achieve a specific goal or objective formulated by the teacher. Questioning strategies have general features, basic formats, and inherent structure. They are limited in number but reflect considerable individual flexibility; a variety of options are available within each to do creative and different things with the related questioning techniques and activities.

While questioning strategies reflect internal flexibility, their overall character and structure are consistent, predictable, and stable.

Questioning techniques are approaches to questioning which incorporate activities chosen selectively to fit the questioning strategy employed in a given lesson. Within a specific questioning strategy, a teacher might opt for a different questioning technique during each of the three phases of a lesson, i.e., one technique for prereading, another for reading, and another for postreading. Note, however, that although it is possible to have different techniques and activities within a given questioning strategy, the strategy chosen imposes certain limitations and restrictions on the technique or techniques chosen.

For example, an effective questioning technique for a number of teaching contexts is that of *devil's advocate questioning*. Students must take certain positions in favor of or in opposition to that of the author in a given text. The students' positions can be either assigned by the teacher or can simply arise through discussion of the text because of the nature of the text itself. When a student states a position, the teacher asks a question designed to point out the limitations of the student's position, or makes a challenging statement that counters the student's position. These questions or statements might be part of a series planned to lead the student into a series of justifications that requires him or her to think carefully about the text.

The devil's advocate questioning technique can be particularly effective with older students in content area classes such as science and social studies. It works best with a persuasive text on a controversial topic. However, it can also be used in the study of fiction. For example, students can defend or challenge actions taken or decisions made by a character in a story. This technique does require excellent classroom rapport between students and between student and teacher.

The teacher may opt for a variety of questioning activities to get the best mileage from this technique; for example, classroom debates, small group discussions to reach consensus on a group position, a writing assignment requiring the students to solidify their positions in a composition, and so on.

This questioning technique and associated activities would probably not be as effective in a questioning strategy geared to establishing an analogy where students relate prior experiences to a totally new subject. (More detail on this questioning strategy will follow.)

We can highlight a few general, important points about questioning strategies, techniques, and activities.

POINT #1

Reading teachers should make a distinction between questioning strategies, questioning techniques, and questioning activities. A questioning strategy is usually an overall questioning approach to all three phases of the reading lesson—prereading, reading, and postreading. It is normally more extended in time than techniques and activities. It has fewer specific attributes but several general features.

POINT #2

Questioning strategies are limited in number compared to questioning techniques and activities.

POINT #3

Questioning strategies should be consistent; predictable.

POINT #4

Questioning techniques are approaches to questioning that incorporate questioning activities. They are used to implement the strategy. Normally, we think of approaches such as semantic mapping, feature analysis, story grammar use, use of questions designed according to a taxonomy, and so on as techniques. A variety of activities involving worksheets, small group discussions, paired work, and so on fit into each of these techniques. It is common in reading education to use these various terms interchangeably, however.

POINT #5

Questioning techniques reflect some limitations imposed by the questioning strategy that has been selected. Questioning techniques and activities should be varied and creative.

POINT #6

Both questioning techniques and activities *must* be chosen so that they fit the strategy to reinforce the overall intent of the reading lesson.

QUESTIONING STRATEGIES

Before addressing specific questioning strategies, we shall note a few important points regarding questioning and instruction in reading comprehension generally.

Effective instruction in reading comprehension is more likely to occur when the teacher sees any given reading lesson as being made up of three important phases—prereading, reading, and postreading. Some researchers believe that most of what is learned during a reading lesson is determined by what takes place during the prereading phase, and, further, that most of the questioning during the postreading phase is largely monitoring in character.

Questions can be put into two different categories regardless of their level on any questioning taxonomy. They are either *instructional* or they are *monitoring*. Instructional questions are those designed to help the student develop effective approaches to reading and thus improve his or her reading comprehension. Monitoring questions are intended to provide the teacher with information about the level or degree of comprehension occurring in the reading of the text.

The most likely time to ask effective instructional questions is in the prereading phase and, to a somewhat lesser extent, the reading phase. In postreading, because the students have already read the text, instructional context dictates that most of the questions will function as monitors even though we may prefer it otherwise.

Therefore, in designing every reading lesson, the three phases of reading instruction must be considered. Some techniques and activities capitalize primarily upon the prereading phase, some upon the reading phase, and some the postreading. The teacher must remember that different kinds of techniques and activities function differently in the different phases of instruction. Some work best during prereading; others best during postreading. Some work only during postreading; others during any of the three phases of the lesson.

Questions asked during prereading play a central role in determining the amount of higher-level thinking the students engage in during the reading. During this period, inferential questions tend to be more productive than lower-level questions or a mix of question types (Hansen and Pearson, 1981; Hansen, 1981; and others). Questions that implicitly pressure the learner to predict possible outcomes are important. Also, questions which encourage learners to connect ideas through analogies are useful in generating suppositional thinking during the text reading. Image-inducing questions can be helpful during the prereading and reading phases for learners who prefer mental imagery as a schema base. Such questions, when well timed, can also be effective in improving the facility for visual learning (Pressley, 1976; Mayer, 1980).

Discussion questions asked during postreading are more effective when they are tied to the prereading phase of instruction (Hansen and Pearson, 1983; Hansen, 1981; and others). To some extent, postreading questions need to be individualized to the student's background knowledge and hypothesizing ability. *Probe questions* should be specifically designed to reinforce hypothesized ideas generated by inferential questions used during the prereading period. For example:

Inferential: Why did William decide to leave the island?
Probe questions for assistance: 1. What happened the night before?
2. How did he feel after the storm?
3. What did he miss that was on the mainland?

With older students, questions should be designed to implicitly pressure the student to think about the differences between answers of *validation* and answers of *verification*. Opinions or conclusions derived from empirical data or physical evidence use a validating process and can thus be identified as being valid or invalid. Opinions derived from nonempirical, nonphysical evidence are more subjective and use a verifying process. Some hypotheses are verifiable; some can be validated.

Questions used as advance organizers should include some general or *gist-type* questions, e.g., "What is the main reason for the separation of powers between the legislative, the executive, and the judicial in the federal government?" The same is true for study guide questions.

Reading teachers must remember that questioning is the heart of comprehension instruction. The success of other instructional efforts is largely dependent upon the success of the teacher's questioning strategies.

Common Characteristics

Despite their differences, questioning strategies have certain characteristics in common. One characteristic is the assumption that the effective reader constantly hypothesizes about the text. What will happen next? Where is the plot leading? What is the point of a particular section of text, a particular paragraph, or even a particular sentence? Predictions are made and tested constantly. The act of reading is an ongoing guessing game with the better reader making educated guesses instead of wild ones.

All questioning strategies assume the reader's ability to reason; to use and apply basic principles of analysis.

Another characteristic of all questioning strategies is that they are dependent upon the reader's background knowledge. Therefore, all questioning strategies include techniques and activities for activating prior knowledge or building background knowledge necessary to read the text effectively. Readers approach this task in different ways, but the ultimate goal is the same, regardless of strategy.

Problem solving

For students to become involved with effective questioning strategies, they must be able to make predictions based upon some hypothesis they have formulated about the text to be read. Further, they must be able to tie these predictions to some sort of hypothesis testing and concluding strategy of their own. In other words, they must be able to approach the task with some degree of problem-solving abilities.

It is important to remember that all human beings have problem-solving approaches—*all*. The difference between their approaches is that some are thought out and formalized, while others are not.

It is also important to note that all learners have problem-solving capacities, from kindergarten children to research scientists. These abilities differ in degree of sophistication, not in kind or process, *if* learners are provided opportunities to develop essential problem-solving skills early on.

Since effective implementation of questioning strategies begins with *prediction* and since prediction is not particularly useful without the ability to test it and draw conclusions, it would appear that students should have some knowledge of a problem-solving process to make most effective use of a questioning strategy.

Although there are a variety of formal problem-solving processes advocated, most have a few basic components in common, which all readers should know and use. Following is a simplified problem-solving outline which fits well with the questioning strategies presented later in this chapter. Steps one to three are normally employed in the prereading phase; Step four during the reading phase; and Step five during the postreading phase in the macro application of the three components to the reading lesson. Steps one to five are applied in micro applications in an ongoing fashion during the actual reading to substantiate supporting details for major points in the text.

Notice that the reader should complete two steps before formulating a hypothesis or, in other words, before making a prediction. First, the reader must identify the problem which will generate the hypothesis, i.e., get a clear grasp of the perimeters and parameters of the subject and a general grasp of probable author intent. This can be done quickly and informally in some cases and must require considerable time and effort in others.

One of the ongoing problems that plagues teachers who attempt to use the prereading phase of instruction productively is the tendency of students to turn the discussion into a brainstorming session without restricting themselves to prior experiences that are relevant to the text. This is where the teacher should be in control. **Do not allow discussion to drift** from subjects relevant to the content of the text during the prereading phase. Training your students in the problem-solving process can help with this.

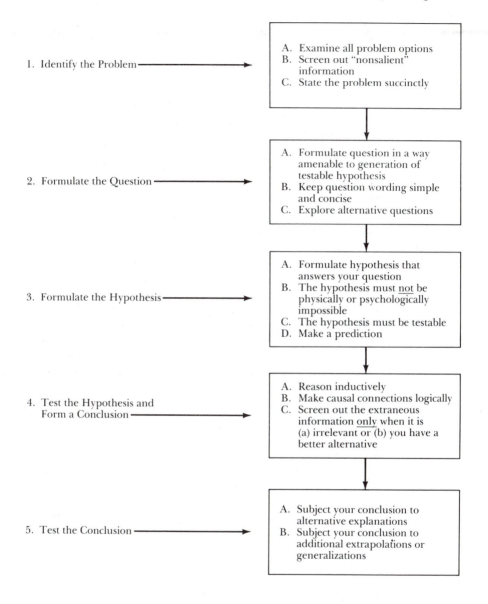

1. Identify the Problem
   - A. Examine all problem options
   - B. Screen out "nonsalient" information
   - C. State the problem succinctly

2. Formulate the Question
   - A. Formulate question in a way amenable to generation of testable hypothesis
   - B. Keep question wording simple and concise
   - C. Explore alternative questions

3. Formulate the Hypothesis
   - A. Formulate hypothesis that answers your question
   - B. The hypothesis must <u>not</u> be physically or psychologically impossible
   - C. The hypothesis must be testable
   - D. Make a prediction

4. Test the Hypothesis and Form a Conclusion
   - A. Reason inductively
   - B. Make causal connections logically
   - C. Screen out the extraneous information <u>only</u> when it is (a) irrelevant or (b) you have a better alternative

5. Test the Conclusion
   - A. Subject your conclusion to alternative explanations
   - B. Subject your conclusion to additional extrapolations or generalizations

Step 1 During the first step of your discussion in the prereading phase, have your students develop a direct statement of the problem, i.e., "The most important problem is . . . ." Be sure students agree that the identified problem is the most important and representative, given the amount of information you have provided them about the text or that they can bring to the discussion.

Step 2   After you and your students have generated possible problem statements, discuss with them how they might ask questions about the problem(s). Write volunteered questions on the board. After you have a reasonable list, with your students attempt to identify the more salient or usable of the questions. Do not simply discard questions, however, without a discussion about their relevance and without generating some explanation for why the questions retained represent better alternatives for use in the reading of the text.

Step 3   Use the same procedure you used in Step two to generate a number of hypotheses based upon the questions. In other words, ask your students to guess possible answers to the questions they have developed. Discuss the possibilities or probabilities of the fruitfulness of their hypotheses, i.e., why or why not for each. Again, discuss the weaknesses of hypotheses or predictions that you decide to discard.

Remember that in the predict-test-conclude questioning strategy (to be discussed), Steps one to three of the problem-solving model will be employed during the prereading phase of instruction. Do not always use the same techniques and activities for this part of your strategy. Remember the potential of paired and small group approaches as well as the different uses of writing by students to generate hypotheses.

Step 4   Hypothesis testing and concluding dominates the reading phase of most questioning strategies. And, although there are a number of excellent techniques for the classroom teacher to enter into the reading phase of the lesson—oral reading, question glossing, question inserting, interrupted silent reading, and so on—the ultimate goal of the reading program is to produce effective silent readers, since that is what most of us will do with our reading during the rest of our lives. That means that our students must master the necessary skills and processes to apply during the actual reading act. Since hypothesis testing is done by applying various reasoning processes, it is critical that students know what these processes are and how and when to employ them in their reading.

Step 5   Although conclusion testing takes place throughout the reading act, it is a key part of most postreading discussions. During this time learners should engage in discussions that allow them to explore alternative possibilities, extend their inferences to new situations, and probe the implications of such extensions.

Reasoning

Although the terms *reasoning* and *thinking* are often used synonymously, they are not the same. Reasoning is a specialized form of thinking. Many types of thinking do not qualify as reasoned thinking, although most, if not all, play important roles in our lives. When one reasons, one consciously applies a fairly structured set of processes to a task to make the most logical decision from among all the possible decisions that could be reached.

Basically, a reader can employ two kinds of reasoning, formal and informal. Formal reasoning consists of *inductive* and *deductive* reasoning. Examples of informal reasoning include reasoning by analogy and reasoning by correlation. These are more directly applicable to a questioning strategy to be discussed later in this chapter. However, it should be noted that just as all grammars "leak," so too does logic. All categories of reasoning leak; they squish over into each other's domains, sometimes assisting, sometimes interfering.

Traditionally, teachers have taught students that inductive reasoning is inferring (concluding) a generalization from a set of particular data. For example, if I observe over a period of time that dogs a,b,c,d . . . all have long hair, then I might infer or conclude that all dogs have long hair. I have reasoned from particular observations to a generalization.

Deductive reasoning, on the other hand and according to traditional definition, goes from general to particular. For example, I note that all automobiles need fuel to operate, and I have just purchased an automobile. I can therefore infer (conclude) that my individual automobile will need fuel to operate also. I have reasoned from a general set of circumstances to a particular or specific one.

Unfortunately, however, these definitions do not hold up under closer scrutiny. Consider this inductive reasoning example:

1. All women I see sometimes wear dresses.
2. All women I see sometimes wear slacks.
3. Therefore, all women I see sometimes wear dresses and sometimes wear slacks.

Notice that we have reasoned from generalizations to another generalization. Or consider this deductive reasoning example:

1. If Jane goes to the movie, she will not be able to go home with Sue Ellen.
2. Jane is going to the movie.
3. Therefore, Jane is not going home with Sue Ellen.

In this case, our deductive reasoning moves from particulars to a conclusion that is also particular.

Although it is true that, most commonly, inductive reasoning moves from a set of particulars to a general conclusion and deductive reasoning moves in the opposite direction, the exceptions preclude suggesting that this is the significant difference between the two modes of reasoning.

In fact the primary and most important difference between inductive and deductive reasoning is that inductive reasoning always involves *extrapolation,* sometimes called *the inductive leap.* That means that the inference is *always* probable, *not* a certainty, even if all the data are true.

We all can think of obvious examples where the probability of being incorrect is pretty small, even infinitesimal. For example, based upon years of daily observation of a,b,c,d . . . x number of people that all wear clothing in public, I project that the next person I see in public will be wearing clothing. I'll most likely be correct in my inductive reasoning. However, my conclusion is not very powerful. Generally, the longer the extrapolation or inductive leap, the more powerful our conclusion, i.e., the more useful and applicable to a wider range of data or problems. The shorter the inductive leap, the less useful our conclusion or inference.

In deductive reasoning, our conclusion is *entailed,* or required by the data in the premises. If we have reasoned validly (accurately) and the data are true, then the conclusion or inference *must* follow; no choice about it!

Reading involves *both* inductive and deductive processes, which often interact during text processing; thus, they are both important. However, there are few instances of actual syllogistic deductive arguments found in most texts. That is, our students will seldom see actual arguments expressed in the deductive mode in text. Most text employs inductive reasoning. However, we are less concerned with the text's mode of reasoning than we are with the reader's use of reasoning during the reading.

When we discuss the predict-test-conclude strategy, we will emphasize the use of reasoning for more effective comprehension of text, no matter what its form or textual mode. During the reading phase, the student must be able to reason effectively enough to test predictions, both those important ones generated in prereading, along with revisions of those made while reading and new predictions developed during the reading act.

Using inductive reasoning appropriately during the reading is probably the most improtant skill incorporated into any questioning strategy. Therefore, some time should be spent with students in developing several inductive approaches to hypothesis testing and inferring.

Inductive Reasoning

Students need to be able to apply a number of inductive reasoning modes in their reading. One is the *method of agreement.*

Suppose that one day after lunch at school, some students become ill. A few of the ill students are interviewed and the following facts are learned:

1. Student Jones: ate soup, ate fish, ate salad, and got ptomaine.

2. Student Smith: ate soup, ate no fish, ate salad, and got ptomaine.
3. Student Williams: ate no soup, ate fish, ate salad, and got ptomaine.

What food caused the ptomaine? How did you reason?

We decide that salad is the culprit by examining the things that the students ate in common; we used the method of agreement.

Another mode of inductive reasoning is the *method of difference.*

Let's return to the school with the dangerous cafeteria where students eat at their own risk. Suppose the next week a number of students again become ill. The following data are collected:

1. Student Otts: ate meat, ate pie, ate ice cream, and got ptomaine.
2. Student Jennings: ate no meat, ate pie, ate no ice cream, and got ptomaine.
3. Student Benson: ate meat, ate no pie, ate no ice cream, and did not get ptomaine.

What food caused the ptomaine? How did you reason?

We conclude that Student Benson avoided ptomaine because this student was the only one who skipped the pie; otherwise the foods eaten overlapped. The pie was the only thing different; we used the *method of difference.*

Let's return one final time to our disastrous school cafeteria. Some students are determined to give it another try. A number more are taken ill and the following data are collected:

1. Student Houser: ate one hamburger and got ptomaine with a fever of 101.
2. Student Jackson: ate two hamburgers and got ptomaine with a temperature of 102.
3. Student James: ate three hamburgers and got ptomaine with a fever of 103.

What kind of conclusion can you infer? There is clearly a correlation between degree of temperature and quantity of the tainted food eaten. This reasoning is called the *method of concomitant variance.* As one set of data vary, a variance occurs proportionately in something else.

In other words, readers skilled in the three inductive modes outlined here would look for similarities, differences, and concomitant relationships in data change as they make decisions about the appropriateness of their predictions and attempt to reach some conclusions in their reading.

It is highly unlikely that any text will be so patterned as to present information to the reader as this information was. However, the three principles of similarity, difference, and concomitant variance are still at work and still useful to the reader in addressing the text, even though the structure of the text and its information are more likely to be much looser and more informal than are the examples we have used here for illustrative purposes. Students should have opportunities to practice these modes in a variety of ways from fairly tight and structured, e.g., solving logical problems and reasoning syllogistically, to more informal.

Causality

Causality is a key element in all phases of a questioning strategy. The reader must be able to look for causal connections regardless of what reasoning modes are applied, either prior to or after the reading begins. Ability to detect specious logic and faulty cause-effect relationships, and to make appropriate cause-effect connections in text, have long been identified as important to reading comprehension.

However, the complexities of causality are many. To begin with, we normally use more than one sense of the term *cause*. For example, I might say, "She wants to be an artist so she can share her insights with the world." We infer from this that her desire to share is the essential cause for her becoming an artist. However, I can also say, "She is a good artist because I saw her paintings in the New York Museum of Modern Art." In this case, my seeing her paintings in the museum did not cause her to be a good artist. Instead, it is evidence for me that she is one; it is a reason for knowing something or for justifying my knowledge about something *rather* than being an actual cause.

Or consider, "He is a bachelor because he is not married." This is not a cause-effect statement either. It is called a *tautology*, a definition. We can reverse the statement and it means the same thing, which we could not do if it were a causal statement.

And if this is not enough to "cause" confusion, there is another sense of cause which appears quite commonly in text our students are asked to read. This is the idea that implies that physical underlying causes are secondary to more relevant surface causes. In this sense, a cause is the incident or action that, in the presence of those conditions which ordinarily exist, made the difference between the occurrence or nonoccurrence of the event. For example, if an insurance investigator is seeking to determine whether or not the burning down of a wooden building is a case of arson, he obviously is not looking for all of the necessary conditions, or sufficient conditions. He is not interested in finding out if oxygen was present or if wood will burn at a certain temperature in the presence of oxygen. The insurance investigator is trying to discover whether or not some human being deliberately started the fire.

Little wonder then that students have difficulty mastering this very important concept necessary for effective reading comprehension!

We should also point out that teachers often contribute to the confusion surrounding the concept of causality by not making necessary distinctions in their use of key words during questioning.

Examine these three related but different questions:

1. Describe how X happened.
2. Explain how X happened.
3. Justify the occurrence of X.

Each of these three questions asks the student to do something different. In question number one, we are simply asking for a straightforward, objective description of what occurred. In question number two, we anticipate that the student will include underlying causes for X's occurrence. In other words, the term *explain* entails an obligation to include causality in the response, which the term *describe* does not.

To justify the occurrence of X, however, requires a rationale for the occurrence of X. Under normal conditions, a question using the term *justify* assumes that the responder will include causality as part of the justification for X. This need not always be the case. If a student has misbehaved in class and you ask the student to explain his or her behavior, you expect the student to address causes in the response. If you ask the student to justify the action, you may or may not get causes in the response, e.g., "I did it because other students have done it, and you never complained," as opposed to "I did it to show off in front of Janet."

So, what are the implications for teachers?

1. Provide a variety of activities for your students designed to teach them the various kinds of causal relationships.
2. Watch the language in your questions to assure more precise use of terms such as *describe, explain, justify,* and so on.
3. Teach your students to examine all data in inductive inference from an *internal* causal perspective, i.e., consider whether X's occurrence with Y is simply correlational or whether it is actually causal.

The Predict-Test-Conclude (PTC) Strategy

The predict-test-conclude (PTC) questioning strategy has a wide range of possible applications. More than any other, it builds from the problem-solving, reasoning, and causality principles that we have discussed. It can be used for both fiction and nonfiction text; for short stories, novels, essays, newspaper articles, persuasive texts, reports, and so on. Because it embodies the most applicable specifics of reading comprehension (which are bound up in reasoning and thinking generally), its application potential is quite extensive. Also, it is not grade-level specific. The level of sophistication can be adjusted to accommodate younger and older learners without changing the components themselves.

The steps of prediction, testing, and concluding represent both macro-process and micro-process applications. In the macro-process application, each of the three steps represents the focus of questioning in each of the three phases of the reading lesson—prereading (predicting), reading (testing), and postreading (concluding). During the prereading phase, questioning encourages students to make predictions about the text to be read. During the reading, they test their predictions, and in the postreading phase, they discuss conclusions based upon the testing of the initial predictions.

In the micro-process application, the strategy encourages learners to apply the three-step process (predict, test, and conclude) throughout all three phases of the lesson, and especially to form predictions and hypotheses which support the larger and more important predictions made.

For the teacher the primary focus of this questioning strategy is on the prereading phase. Although there are a number of things which are done during the other two phases, as we shall note, the most important instruction takes place during the prereading phase.

PTC in Prereading

Questions asked during this phase of instruction should be designed to encourage the learner to hypothesize about the text before seeing it. There are certain stock phrases that tend to introduce questions that help the student hypothesize.

"If X happens when Y is present, what results?"

"If you were going to read a story (article) about X, what are some of the things you think might occur?"

"When X happens, what usually takes place?"

"Imagine you are in X situation with a, b, and c conditions, what would you do?"

"How would you respond to X if you were forced to do so?"

These questions tend to be if-then, or conditional, questions that ask the student to take a position. Generally, if-then statements and questions are very complex and quite possibly the most logically difficult structures in the English language for students to master. Piaget observed little use of such constructions and very limited mastery of their basics through ten and eleven years of age. Klein found little sophisticatioon prior to those ages and little if any refinement even with seventeen year olds (Klein, 1973).

This is not to suggest that our questioning strategy, which relies heavily upon initial questioning that uses this and closely related structures, should be reserved for older students. But it does mean that the classroom teacher employing the PTC strategy must be prepared to paraphrase and work around the technical difficulties of logically correct inferences from the conditional. Even kindergarten children can reason inferentially, however, and with appropriate modifications of language and detail, this strategy can be used at any grade level (Klein, 1973; 1976).

Another observation which can be made about the questions used during the prereading phase is that they always require the student to use background knowledge in answering. That means that if background knowledge is lacking, time and effort must be given to building the necessary knowledge before proceeding. For the most part, if materials to be read have been chosen carefully, most students should have at least the minimum knowledge necessary to make predictions about the text.

STEPS FOR PTC STRATEGY IN PREREADING

1. Carefully read the text prior to class. Identify the most important conclusions that you feel the reader must infer from the reading to get the gist of the text. Note those for yourself.
2. Think of at least three important questions that would encourage students to hypothesize about likely outcomes of events or activities in the text, e.g., if-then questions.
3. Think of necessary suggestions, ideas, or additional questions you might need to bring to the surface students' background knowledge, or different ways you can generate necessary, *new* knowledge for them. In many instances the latter can be done by using probe questions to find out what your students know about the text's subject or closely related subjects. This can be an excellent opportunity to use peer teaching: you can pair up students; use small groups; or within large class discussion allow students with the necessary prior experience to help build background knowledge for the other students.

   In other instances, it might be just as easy for you to provide either an oral or written overview or outline of the text with appropriate comments—an advance organizer of sorts, if you will.
4. Have your students write down predictions based upon their responses to your questions. These will later be used during the reading phase as benchmarks to test their hypotheses.*
5. Close the prereading phase with discussion of written predictions and students' rationale for them.

PTC in Reading and Postreading

After the prereading phase, students should be well prepared to test their predictions during the reading, alter them if necessary, and generate new ones as they go along. The teacher really has only a couple of options here: you can let the students read silently or let them read orally. In either

---

*Note that in nearly all components of reading instruction, we ask students to write. This use of writing in all phases of instruction and in all reading contexts is intended to demonstrate how writing can be integrated into the reading lesson, rather than being attached to it. Note the chapter on the reading/writing connection for further suggestions on this point.

case, you have another two choices: you can either interrupt their reading at selected times or not.

Interrupted reading can be beneficial if used judiciously and quite selectively. You can monitor individual student progress as well as ask appropriate additional questions to help the student in hypothesis generation and prediction testing. Used too often, it can lead to readers who miss the gestalt, the meaning of the whole which comes with particular kinds of text, such as poetry; readers who become over-the-shoulder-lookers wondering when you are going to interrupt again with more questions.

Use this technique selectively and carefully!

Another form of interrupted reading uses study sheets or pages containing the text with questions written in the margins, usually with chunks of appropriate text bracketed (glossing).

These activities, too, should be used selectively.

Questioning during the postreading phase keys back to important questions raised during the prereading phase. Questioning should begin with higher-level inferential questions related to hypotheses generated in the prereading. If students have difficulty responding, then lower-level *probe* questions can be used. These probe questions should help students pinpoint salient facts, events, or other data sources necessary to see causal connections and to draw the appropriate inferences entailed in the higher-level questions.

If done effectively, discussion will probably center on the various conclusions reached during the reading. Therefore, as with the prereading phase, you must work to keep the discussion on track and relevant to the text.

HIGHLIGHTS OF THE PTC STRATEGY

1. During prereading, help students identify an appropriate problem area and questions associated with it.
2. During this phase, use questioning that encourages students to formulate hypotheses or predictions about what is likely to take place—benchmarks they can use to guide their reading.
3. During the reading, selectively use interrupted questions or study aids of text with inserted or glossed questions.
4. During postreading, design questions which key back to those posited during the prereading. Tie the discussion to the ideas generated in prereading.
5. Use probe questions to help students make causal connections or draw inferences.

Techniques and Activities

Both here and in the remainder of this chapter where teaching techniques and activities are suggested to improve reading comprehension through questioning, remember that virtually all of these can be used in any of a variety of questioning strategies. To some extent the placement of them here is arbitrary. However, as you examine them, you should see some special applicability to the PTC questioning strategy.

● Prepare a handout such as the following and distribute it to students during the prereading phase.

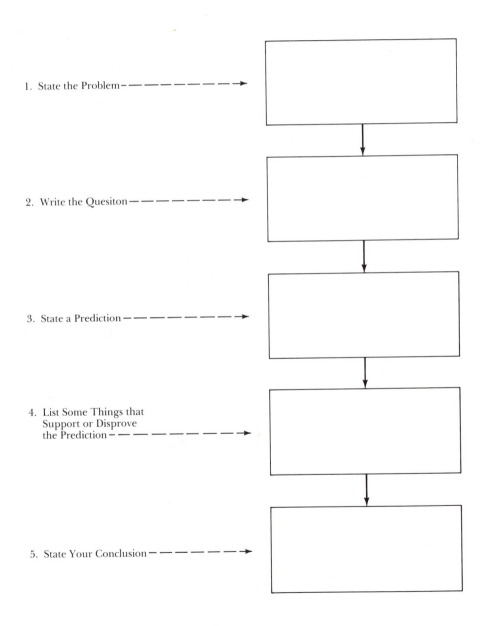

1. State the Problem – — — — — — — ➤

2. Write the Quesiton — — — — — — ➤

3. State a Prediction — — — — — — ➤

4. List Some Things that
   Support or Disprove
   the Prediction – — — — — — — — ➤

5. State Your Conclusion — — — — — ➤

Have your students fill out the first three boxes during the prereading discussions. Ask them to use the handout during the reading and complete the remaining boxes. You may wish to use more than one handout per student so that they can write separate predictions on each one.

The primary purpose of this activity is to get students into the habit of going through the problem-solving steps that are important for hypothesis formulation and testing.

● Find short articles from the newspaper—two to three paragraphs—on things such as fires, burglaries, auto accidents, and so on. These are especially productive since they typically have easily identifiable causes. Retype the articles, duplicate them for handout, and ask students to find causes and effects.

● Provide students with hypotheses. Have them indicate how they would go about testing them. For example:

1. Redheads have terrible tempers.
2. Running is good for your health.
3. We need a new school building.
4. You get what you pay for.
5. Cows usually lie down when it rains.
6. Working in a coal mine is bad for your health.

You can vary the difficulty of this task by the kind of generalization you select for testing. For older students, you will want to include some that are quite challenging, e.g., "The more paying freight you load aboard a cargo plane, the greater the profit earned from the flight will tend to be." Application of a version of the method of concomitant variance might be called for here.

As a prereading activity, formulate generalizations about the text to be read. These can be used as benchmarks for student discussion or during application of associated activities in prereading.

● Present students with examples of reasoning fallacies and ask them to identify faults, i.e., what has been assumed, what has not been considered, what has been given too much weight in the reasoning, and so on. For example, the following represent possibilities for a range of grades:

1. The western half of the United States is all very dull and boring. I know, because I once spent a weekend with my sister in Kansas City.
2. Murderers are always discovered, sooner or later. Just think back. When did you ever hear of a murder that hadn't been discovered?
3. I interviewed fifty students in the lounge of the student union at the college. I asked them whether they preferred to study in a noisy place. Thirty-five of

them said, yes, that they disliked quiet and enjoyed studying in noisy, bustling places. I infer that the majority of students do not like to study where it is quiet.

4. One August afternoon in my garden I set up an insect trap that has a fan to suck in the insects. After operating the trap for one hour, I emptied out the dead insects, sorted, and counted them. Although there were hundreds of insects, the only large ones were butterflies and grasshoppers. I infer that there probably are no large moths in this region during August.

Include examples of faulty reasoning on topics or issues in the students' text.

● Present your students with brief, introductory summaries of prospective texts. For example, you might survey your basal reader or subject matter textbook for appropriate examples. Have your students do two things:

1. Make predictions that are warranted.
2. Tell how they will test the predictions and what they will accept as evidence.

   Example: This story is about two young boys who go for a hike along the beach in search of lost treasure. They find an old abandoned beach shack and explore inside. They find a surprise. The rest of the story is about how they get back to their homes.

When used prior to reading the selection, this device can be a powerful motivator as well as an excellent technique for developing necessary reasoning skills for effective comprehension.

● Give students the titles of some stories or selections they will be reading soon. With no information other than the titles, have them write brief paragraphs for each, indicating what they think the text will be about.

● Prepare *quantified* reasoning problems for your students and ask them to choose the most *logical* possible conclusion that can be inferred. For example:

Some new cars are troublesome for their owners.

We have just bought a new car.

Therefore:

a. We will have a troublesome car.

b. We will not have a troublesome car.

c. We might have a troublesome car.

After they have had practice choosing from alternatives that you have provided, ask students to infer their own conclusion. For example:

Sometimes new bicycles have problems.

I have a new bike.

Therefore: _____

_____

_____

Tie this activity to the text by constructing syllogisms using actual text characters, events, problems, and so on.

The Analogize-Fit-Infer (AFI) Strategy

It is difficult to teach a reading lesson when your students have limited or no background knowledge or prior experience with the subject matter. This problem is more common in the earlier grades; as students mature, they have more and more experiences that provide background knowledge for their reading. Nonetheless, it can be a problem at any grade level and represents a serious challenge for the teacher of reading.

When it is a problem, analogize-fit-infer (AFI) questioning strategy can be most helpful. Regardless of limited prior experience, all students share certain life experiences.

Suppose you will be reading a selection from your social studies text with a group of sixth graders. For the first time they will be introduced to the concept of balance of powers in the federal government. The text examines the structures of the legislative, executive, and judicial branches. In addition, and most importantly for the first reading assignment in the chapter and on this topic, the text focuses upon the division of powers between the branches of government. It gives considerable attention to the reasons our forefathers wrote such power divisions into the Constitution. The Supreme Court as arbiter in situations of disagreement is a key theme.

Assume that none of your students have any background in the subject. What are some things you can do during the prereading to prepare them for the text?

Establishing an analogous connection between the subject of the upcoming reading and something they know and have experienced is probably the most logical thing to do. Consider the following possible scenario:

TEACHER: How many of you have brothers or sisters?
           (Hands go up.)
           Jimmie, tell us about your sister. How old is she, what does she like to do, how do the two of you get along?

JIMMIE: Her name's JoAnn and she's in the seventh grade. She goes to school here at Wilson, too.

TEACHER: Yes, I had JoAnn in class when she was in the fourth grade, also. She's really nice.

JIMMIE: Yeah, most of the time, I guess.

TEACHER: You guess! Don't tell me that JoAnn and you sometimes disagree!

JIMMIE: You kidding! You oughta have her for a sister. She always wants things her way.

TEACHER: Oh, I see. Sometimes the two of you don't agree, is that it?

JIMMIE: Yeah.

TEACHER: Can you think of a time when you disagreed about something and, even though you had to reach a decision, you couldn't?

JIMMIE: Well, just last week. Mom and Dad said that they had the weekend off, so we could either go to Grandma and Grandpa's to visit, or we could stay home and go to the beach for a picnic and then go to a movie.

TEACHER: Well, that doesn't sound like a problem. Either one sounds fun.

JIMMIE: Yes, but I have a neat friend in Lexington where my grandparents live, and I wanted to see him. You can go to the dumb beach anytime!

TEACHER: And, what about JoAnn? What did she want to do?

JIMMIE: Oh, she wanted to go to the beach, naturally! She just likes to show off for the guys!

TEACHER: Well, did you try to talk things out, consider the advantages and disadvantages of both things?

JIMMIE: Yeah, but that didn't do any good. We just couldn't agree.

TEACHER: So what did you do?

JIMMIE: Well, Mom and Dad had to decide for us.

TEACHER: That's too bad. I mean too bad that JoAnn and you could not come to agreement this time. I know both of you, so I bet that you do agree most of the time.

Class, notice how even two nice people like JoAnn and Jimmie cannot always agree. They have to have Mom and Dad help them come to agreement sometimes.

We are going to be reading a new chapter in our social studies book for tomorrow. It is about our federal government and how it operates.

Just think about how large our country is and how many different parts there are to it and what a huge job it is to run it!

Also, think about all of the different people involved in our government and how they can't always agree—like JoAnn and Jimmie don't always agree.

Our textbook is going to tell us about the three basic parts of our federal government—the Congress, the President, and the Supreme Court. The President and the Congress often disagree on what is best for the country. Sometimes, in fact, after a lot of talk and attempts to get together they just can't. Sometimes the Supreme Court has to step in and help. Or, sometimes the President or the Congress might want to do something that goes beyond their authority. The Supreme Court again steps in and makes a decision based on our Constitution. While you read, I want you to think about why we have three main parts in the federal government and think about how JoAnn and Jimmie and how you and your brother or sister or friend agree on things and how things get decided in your family.

The division of federal governmental powers is a very abstract concept. It is difficult enough for adults to grasp, much less grade-school children. In this scenario to establish an analogy for the reading, the teacher attempts to draw upon experiences that all the children are likely to have had and can relate to.

Notice that the analogy is loose; there is not a one-on-one correspondence between the components of sibling conflict and the decision-making system of the federal government. When trying to establish an analogous situation for the reader to tie into, we will seldom be able to make a tight fit. However, we are not that concerned with the formal logic of analogies here, but with creating a connection in the reader that is personal and relevant.

Question types for the prereading phase tend to be interpretation, analysis, and application questions. For example:

"Tell me some things you can say about X." (X should be the analogous referent for Y, which is central in the text.)

"How is A like B?" (Where A and B are events or ideas students know and where both their attributes *and* relationship to each other correspond somewhat to X and Y which are in the text. X and Y can be characters or events in a story, conditions or circumstances in nonfiction, e.g., persuasive essay, newspaper editorial, and so on).

"What are some things you dislike about Z?" (Where Z bears a strong similarity to Q which is in the text.)

"What are some things you like about Z?" (Where Z bears a strong similarity to Q which is in the text.)

"Can you think of a time when nothing seemed to go right for you? Let's list the things that went wrong for you. Let's also think of some reasons why things might have gone wrong for you." (Useful when a story to be read has a main character who is feeling down on himself or herself because others are angry with him or her, or some other factor or set of factors is at play.)

The usefulness of this questioning strategy is determined in large measure by the teacher's knowledge of individual students, including their personal interests, circumstances, likes, dislikes, and so on. Compared to the predict-test-conclude strategy, the AFI strategy is far more personal and direct. One could imagine, theoretically, how the first strategy might be used with a class of students we did not know, whereas the AFI strategy is tied directly to classroom rapport and our familarity with our students.

During the actual reading, the teacher acts as a question-and-cue facilitator to help the reader keep the established analogy in mind. We want the reader to think about the degree of fit between the analogous components and relationships and those in the text itself.

The same basic techniques and activities employed in the predict-test-conclude strategy can be used with the AFI strategy. Inserted questions, interrupted reading, study guide outlines or questions, and so on apply, to focus the learner's attention on analogous connections.

The same is true with the postreading period. Here the teacher will use questions that implicitly pressure the student to make judgmental inferences regarding the validity of the initial analogy or analogies established during the prereading phase. Questions such as the following are natural for the postreading phase:

"Did you think that X in the story was like the Y we talked about before you read it? How were they alike? How were they different?"

"What were some similarities you found between X and Y in the story that were like the similarities we discussed between A and B?"

"What would you say is the biggest difference between P and Q, who were in the story, and R and S that we talked about?"

"Now that you have read this text, can you think of a better comparison we can make for Z than the one we suggested with W earlier?"

All postreading questions in this strategy require the learner to refer back to questions posited during the prereading and reading phases of instruction.

Remember! An important key to effective questioning strategies is that the questions asked during any of the three phases of instruction can be related to other questions in the strategy. Questions asked during postreading find their justification in the questions which were asked during the prereading phase of instruction.

HIGHLIGHTS OF THE AFI STRATEGY

1. The AFI strategy establishes a comparison model for the reader, who can then think, "A is to B (stuff I know) as C is to D (stuff I am going to be reading about)."

2. With the AFI strategy, the teacher must know his or her students and their backgrounds and must have excellent rapport with the class.

3. Questions always require students to think in terms of relationships, i.e., A is to B as C is to something else.

4. The analogies established in this strategy need *not* be logically right, just instructionally satisfying (the teacher senses when students make a close enough connection for the reading to be successful).

5. Any questioning used during the actual act of reading must keep the students' focus on analogous relationships established during the prereading.

6. Questions asked during the postreading are keyed to those asked during the prereading.

Techniques and Activities

Thinking analagously can be quite challenging. (Some of us can recall the infamous "Millers" from our graduate school days!) To make best use of the AFI Strategy, students must have some experience with analogies so that they will know what they are and how they are used.

We should note immediately that one cannot prove anything logically by analogy. It is an informal method of logic which lacks the validating strengths of inductive and deductive reasoning. However, analogies can be powerful describers and can provide us with important comparison insights not possible otherwise.

Analogies have varying degrees of fit. If I say, "1 is to 2 as A is to B," I have made a fairly tight analogical statement. The sequence of like symbols in the first part of our analogy is the same as the sequence of like symbols in the second half. If I say, "1 is to A as 2 is to B," I have made an even tighter analogical fit, for not only am I suggesting a sequencing correspondence, but I am also suggesting something about the relationship between two separate symbol systems.

Since analogies are essentially comparison devices, they are related to other devices in our language which we use for comparison, namely similes and metaphors, which are often described in terms of their analogizing capacities. In fact, in a subtler form of the AFI model, the teacher establishes an underlying metaphor during the prereading phase; the reader then uses the analogical ties between the dominant metaphor and elements of the text being read.

In any event, the ability to work with analogies—to analogize word and concept relationships and to look at two different notions, A and B, to see common attributes—makes a better, more insightful reader.

Here are some ideas for getting your students prepped for the AFI strategy.

• Provide students with a number of objects—for example, apple, orange, plum—and ask them to identify all the similarities and differences that exist amongst the objects that they can think of. Notice how the complexity of the task can be varied by throwing in more objects. While the fruits suggested here might be relatively easy, if you include rock in the group, the task becomes more difficult.

• Provide students with analogies to complete. Move them progressively through more complex analogies, where they must examine an increasing number of relationships before making the connection necessary. For example:

Step I

Black is to *white* as *hard* is to *steel - stone - solid - soft - blue.*

or,

Wheel - engine - hoot - four - horn is to *car* as *bell* is to *bicycle.*

or,

Horse is to *mare - donkey - foal - steer - bull* as *cow* is to *calf.*

Although the position of the term to be selected for the analogy varies, only one term can be chosen. The reader must learn when to hold what in short-term memory.

Step II

Lion is to *lair* as *set - burrow - dog* is to *rabbit - fox - kennel.*

or,

Woman - flower - cow is to *lion - yard - girl* as *tree* is to *bush.*

In analogies of this type, students must keep a number of possible relationships in mind.

Step III

Milk - calf - large is to *cow* as *lamb* is to *wool - little - sheep.*

Think of others. Better yet, have your students think of their own.

● Advertising in magazines, newspapers, radio, and television is an excellent source of analogies. Most advertisers attempt to key their product into some important drive or desire of the consumer. Often they do this by establishing analogous situations or object or events, sometimes directly and sometimes subtly.

Have students analyze advertising for analogies that the advertisers are trying to establish. For example: "Drink Zesty soft drink. It is sprightly enough to make you want to go running!" If aimed at an older audience, the connection with youth and vigor is obvious. Or consider:

> The huge cat turned, eyes drilling into me as I felt the sweat in the palms of my hands. Slowly, very slowly, he turned and walked back into the under-growth. My finger let up on the trigger of the rifle as I shook—visibly!
>
> Later that day, we relaxed by the poolside of the Lake Asenya Hotel and sipped everyone's favorite whiskey, John Evans' Best, and relived the day's experience.

What kind of analogies does the advertiser of this whiskey want the reader to make? Discuss their validity or appropriateness.

Constructing analogical problems using actual characters or events from a text to be read and having students work through them orally in writing, individually, in pairs, or as a class, can be an excellent prereading activity to support your AFI strategy.

The Summarizing-Monitoring-Summarizing (SMS) Strategy

A third questioning strategy, the summarize-monitor-summary (SMS) strategy, is clearly the most teacher-dominated. In particular the teacher commands the prereading phase and student involvement is quite limited.

The teacher initiates the strategy by preparing a summary or an outline of the text to be read. If the text is a content area text and includes sections with titles and subtitles, the summary is built around them instead of using a handout or other material. If the selection is from a tradebook or basal reader and there are ample text adjuncts, i.e., pictures, photographs, graphs, charts, and so on, use them in discussing the text in summary form. Whichever method the teacher employs, the student receives a summary of the text during the prereading.

During this phase the teacher asks questions that focus student attention upon both the main ideas or theses of the text and upon the kind of supporting detail that the student should look for.

To some extent the questions here are similar to those in the predicting-testing-concluding strategy: they help learners hypothesize and test. However, here the instruction is much more direct and deductive, rather than inductive. It encourages students to infer on their own and from their past experience as much as possible.

Examples of questions used in the SMS strategy include:

"Joe, X is the main idea of the story you are going to read. What are some things you think might occur to support this or prove this?"

"Jan, let's skim through the subtitles of our chapter in the social studies book we'll be reading. What do you think the main point of this chapter will be?"

"Bill, you've read this summary of the science chapter selection we'll be reading. Pick out some subsections in the chapter that you think will be less important and let's talk about them."

During the reading, students should use the handout provided to monitor their own reading. For nonfiction, you might want to identify the page number or subsection title where main points or supporting detail are to be found. The summary prepared in the prereading becomes the ongoing literal map the student uses during the reading itself.

In the postreading phase, questions again focus upon summarization. For example:

"What was the main idea of this selection, again, Sandy?"

"Do you agree with Sandy, MaryAnn?"

"Do you think the main points we summarized in the prereading were the best ones? Did we leave any out? Are there some we included which really aren't that important?"

"Henry, in your own words, give us a brief summary of the story."

Because of its structure, the student/teacher roles in the SMS questioning strategy are more limited than in other strategies discussed in this chapter. Among its disadvantages are:

- Students have limited involvement.
- It will not apply to all forms of text; e.g., it is much more effective with nonfiction.
- It provides less motivating power.
- It works more effectively with older students (middle grades, secondary grades).
- It provides fewer alternatives for techniques and activities during the reading phase.

Among the advantages are:

- It is less time-consuming than most other strategies.
- It requires less background knowledge to work well.
- Its *advance organizer* character makes it more useful for later review of material.
- It helps develop the necessary study skills that are important in later grades.

Additional Questioning Strategies, Techniques, and Activities

Following are a number of additional ideas for improving reading comprehension though effective questioning. Many of these are described by their developers or other reading educators as *strategies* when we would probably consider them *techniques*. In those instances where they appear to be techniques rather than instructional strategies, the reader should be able to see how they could be either expanded and further developed into strategies or how they could fit into a strategy already available.

In any event, these teaching ideas have been useful in a wide variety of teaching contexts and in a number of different kinds of reading programs.

The QAR and Its Modifications

Pearson and Johnson are often given credit for the question-answer-relationship (QAR) approach (Pearson and Johnson, 1978). They proposed a simplified questioning taxonomy with only three levels of questions:

1. Text-Explicit Questions: Questions whose answers can be found directly and explicitly in the text, typically word-for-word. These are usually factual recall questions.

2. Text-Implicit Questions: Questions whose answers can be found in the text, but not as obviously as text-explicit answers. Commonly there are no direct grammatical or semantic cues to the answer.

3. Scriptally Implicit Questions: Questions whose answers require use of prior knowledge along with information explicitly provided in the text.

Consider this brief passage:

In 1492 Columbus and his crew sailed from Europe in search of the New World. He commanded three ships on the voyage, the Pinta, the Nina, and the Santa Maria.

After the journey, they landed in America, probably somewhere in Central America, although scholars are not absolutely sure precisely where.

Eventually, he left part of his crew here, and he returned to Spain in hopes of getting more money.

Now, consider the following questions:

1. When did Columbus discover America?
   (In 1492.) This is a text-explicit question. The reader can find the answer directly within a sentence of the text.

2. Why did Columbus leave part of his crew here?
   (Probably to start a settlement or to lay claim to the New World in a formal fashion.) This is a text-implicit question. The reader can likely infer the answer because he is told that Columbus was returning to Spain in order to acquire more money, although the reason for the crew's remaining is not explicitly stated.

3. Was Columbus frightened on his journey to the New World?
   (Probably, given the circumstances and conditions at the time.) This is a scriptally implicit question. There is no indication in the text, direct or implied, about Columbus's feelings. The reader must rely upon background knowledge of the period to infer the answer.

The teacher can use this taxonomy in a variety of ways to more effectively develop reading comprehension skills in the students:

- Use it as a taxonomy to guide questions during all phases of a questioning strategy.
- Teach the taxonomy to students and then have them identify the QAR type they are employing in a given reading lesson (Pearson and Raphael, 1982).
- Have students categorize questions in their textbooks according to the taxonomy; have them practice writing questions of each type for their classmates, using text to be read in class.

Story Grammar Questions

During the past decade or so, there has been an increased interest in applying *story grammars* to the teaching of reading comprehension. Just as individual sentences have structure or internal systems, so, too, do stories.

And, just as different grammarians disagree on what is the best or most accurate grammar available to describe the structure of sentences (we have traditional grammar, structural grammar, transformational grammar, case grammar, and probably many others), different reading authorities have developed different story grammars, e.g., Stein, and others.

Regardless of differences in detail, certain common elements appear in all, e.g., setting, protagonist/anatagonist, initiating event(s), plot development, problem(s), resolution of problem(s), ending, and so on.

A typical story grammar is offered by Stein and Glenn (1979). Here it is with an example of a well-formed story to exemplify each of the elements of the grammar:

1. Setting. Introduction of the protagonist; can contain information about physical, social, or temporal context in which the remainder of the story occurs.

> Example: Once there was a big gray fish named Albert. He lived in a big icy pond near the edge of a forest. One day, Albert was swimming around the pond.

2. Initiating Event. An action, an internal event, or a natural occurrence which serves to initiate or to cause a response in the protagonist.

> Example: Then he spotted a big juicy worm on top of the water. Albert knew how delicious worms tasted.

3. Internal Response. An emotion, cognition, or goal of the protagonist.

> Example: He wanted to eat that one for his dinner. So he swam very close to the worm.

4. Attempt. An overt action to obtain the protagonist's goal.

> Example: Then he bit into him. Suddenly, Albert was pulled through the water into a boat.

5. Consequence. An event, action, or end which marks the attainment or nonattainment of the protagonist's goal.

> Example: He had been caught by fisherman. Albert felt sad.

6. Reaction. An emotion, cognition, action, or end expressing the protagonist's feelings about his goal attainment or relating the broader consequential realm of the protagonist's goal attainment.

> Example: He wished he had been more careful.

Advocates of a questioning strategy based on a story grammar suggest that *Wh* questions be developed to focus students' attention on the story grammar elements. The teacher then would be able to more effectively guide students' thinking through the important elements of the story structure, something that effective readers need to do.

Following are examples of questions based upon the Stein and Glenn story grammar (Klein, 1986):

Where does the story take place? (setting)

What is the first important thing that happens in this story? (initiating event)

What does the main character want to accomplish? (internal response)

How does the main character go after his goal? (attempt)

Does the main character achieve the goal? (consequence)

How does the main character feel at the end of the story? (reaction)

A similar approach with a slightly different story grammar is proposed by Singer and Donlan (1982). Their grammar focuses students' attention upon the leading character, the goal, the obstacles to achieving the goal, the outcome, and the theme of the story.

The various story grammar approaches focus the reader's attention on the important structural and content elements of a story, the elements which are important for the story's flow. They are helpful to learners with limited sense of story grammar and how it relates to the story's meaning, such as children in the primary grades whose parents have done little or no story reading to the children.

In more advanced grades, story-grammar-based questioning strategies are helpful for students who have missed, for whatever reasons, the development of story grammar sense and cannot tie together the various actions and developments in a story.

A FINAL NOTE

In this chapter, I have attempted to provide an overview of the more important aspects of questioning strategies, including a consideration of a selected number of effective questioning strategies appropriate for use in a variety of classrooms and in a variety of grades. As we consider the importance of questioning for reading comprehension instruction, however, there are a couple of additional points that should be made.

Questions never operate in isolation. Any given question asked during a discussion in a reading class dictates both the most likely answer for the context *and* the nature of the question that is likely to follow. The factors that determine the success or failure of any given questioning strategy, in fact, are nearly infinite in number. For instance, there are the normal language discourse patterns of individual classrooms. These are determined by other factors such as individual personalities, classroom environment, teaching philosophy, including theories of learning, and so on. These factors aside, however, the interaction patterns within given questioning strategies are quite complex.

Armbruster et al. (1983), for example, have developed a comprehensive taxonomy of question types that is useful in teaching social studies comprehension. They identified eight categories of question types:

Time (When?)
Location (Where?)
Quantity (How many? and so on)
Name (What or Who?)
Concept Identification (What or Which?)
Explanation (Why?)
Description (What?)
Comparison (Compare/Contrast)

In addition, they elaborated on possible or likely feedback and reaction patterns suggested within each category. Their approach is too detailed to present here, but their attention to the response patterns that hold in particular subject areas and with different questioning strategies suggests that more happens in a discussion using a chosen questioning strategy than we typically realize. Some, such as Jones (1985), advocate the need for more attention to this area and suggest *response instruction* as part of the questioning strategy.

Reading educators such as these have helped point out the limitations of many contemporary approaches to questioning in reading. Much of what we do still results from a sort of spontaneity of the context. Teachers still need to be more precise in the *language of questioning*, and students need to be more aware of question types, the need for greater precision in using questions, responding to them, and thinking about them while reading.

Meanwhile, our efforts need to be the best possible with what we know and what we have available.

ADDITIONAL SELECTED READINGS

DEVINE, T. G. (1986). *Teaching reading comprehension: From theory to practice.* Boston: Allyn and Bacon.
HARRIS, T. L. AND COOPER, E. J. (Eds.) (1985). *Reading, thinking, and concept development: Strategies for the classroom.* New York: College Entrance Examination Board.
IRWIN, J. W. (1986). *Teaching reading comprehension processes.* Englewood Cliffs, N.J.: Prentice-Hall.

KLEIN, M. (1986). *Reading comprehension and the classroom teacher.* Oklahoma City, Ok.: The Economy Company/McGraw-Hill School Division.
PEARSON, P. D. AND JOHNSON, D. (1978). *Teaching reading comprehension.* New York: Holt, Rinehart and Winston.

REFERENCES

ARMBRUSTER, B., ANDERSON, T., et al. (1983). What did you mean by that question? A taxonomy of American history questions (Reading Education Report no. 308). Urbana, Ill.: Center for the Study of Reading.
BOWMAN, J. (1981). The effect of story structure questioning upon the comprehension and metacognitive awareness of sixth grade students. Unpublished doctoral dissertation, University of Maryland.
CUNNINGHAM, J. AND TIERNEY, R. (1984). Research of teaching reading comprehension. In P. D. Pearson (Ed.), *Handbook of reading research.* New York: Longman.
ELLIS, J. (1982). Comparative effects of adjunct postquestions and instructions on learning from text. *Journal of Educational Psychology, 74,* 860-867.
HANSEN, J. (1981). The effects of inference training and practice on young children's reading comprehension. *Reading Research Quarterly, 16,* 391-417.
HANSEN, J. AND PEARSON, P. D. (1983). An institutional study: Improving the inferential comprehension of fourth grade good and poor readers. *Journal of Educational Psychology, 75,* 821-829.
JONES, B. F. (1985). Response instruction. In T. Harris and E. Cooper (Eds.), *Reading, thinking & concept development.* New York: College Entrance Examination Board.
KLEIN, M. (1973). Inferring from the conditional. Unpublished doctoral dissertation, University of Wisconsin.
KLEIN, M. (1986). *Reading comprehension and the classroom teacher.* Oklahoma City, Ok.: The Economy Company/McGraw-Hill School Division.
KLEIN, M. (1976). *Talk in the language arts classroom.* Urbana, Ill.: NCTE/ERIC.
MAYER, R. C. (1980). Elaboration techniques that increase the meaningfulness of technical text: An experimental test of the learning strategy hypothesis. *Journal of Educational Psychology, 72,* 770-784.
PEARSON, P. D. AND JOHNSON, D. (1978). *Teaching reading comprehension.* New York: Holt, Rinehart & Winston.
PEARSON, P. D. AND RAPHAEL, T. (1982). The effect of metacognitive training on children's question-answering behavior (Tech. Rep. No. 238) Urbana: University of Illinois, Center for the Study of Reading.
PRESSLEY, G. M. (1976). Mental imagery helps eight-year-olds remember what they read. *Journal of Educational Psychology, 68,* 355-359.
SINGER, H. AND DONLAN, D. (1982). Active comprehension: Problem-solving schema with question generation for comprehension of complex short stories. *Reading Research Quarterly, 17,* 166-187.
STEIN, N. AND GLENN, C. (1979). An analysis of story comprehension in elementary school children. In R. O. Freedle (Ed.), *New directions in discourse processing.* Hillsdale, N.J.: Erlbaum Assoc.

3

Teaching Reading Vocabulary

SOME OBSERVATIONS

Vocabulary is an important key to effective reading comprehension. Although reading authorities disagree on many particulars of reading acquisition, this is one thing they do agree on—or is it? Certainly all of us in reading education, whatever our capacity, agree that vocabulary is important to reading. Many authorities even think it is critical to all thought (Vygotsky, 1962). Vygotsky argued that the locus of all meaning was the word. Although some word parts, such as prefixes, suffixes, and so on (linguists call these *bound morphemes*), are meaning-bearing units of the language, most linguists concede that when it *really* comes down to meaning, "the *word* is the thing."

Unfortunately, there are a number of unanswered questions about words as a group, not to mention those that qualify as reading vocabulary. For example, we do not know how many words there are (at least partly due to the fact that much of the time we cannot agree on what a word is or isn't). Most estimates of the English language place the volume at 750,000 words or more, i.e., about three fourths of a million. However, we estimate that most speakers, writers, and readers use only 10,000 or so. In fact, about 90% of the vocabulary most of us use during our lives comes from a collection of about 10,000 words. Further, a majority of the words that we use consistently comes from a body of only 5,000 to 7,000 words.

Given these facts, we can all agree that we have personal ownership of only an extremely small number of words available to us from a large vocabulary. Part of the reason for this may be our ongoing desire for conciseness. In our busy, information-laden lives, keeping our vocabulary within the confines of a small personal dictionary has much appeal, if limitations.

However, part of the reason for our extremely limited ownership vocabularies could be the result of ineffective methods of teaching vocabulary. Certainly, there remains considerable disagreement on the specifics of this matter in reading education. To be fair to reading educators, however, we must acknowledge that there are a variety of other factors which can, and probably do to some extent, account for our limited vocabularies.

Given the idiosyncracies of our spelling and pronounciation systems and given the importance that language plays in people's perception of us, most of us are reluctant to venture into the risky domains of writing and public speaking. Even if I do know what the word *halcyon* means when I read it, how in the world do I pronounce it? So what if *cacophony* sounds neat and expresses an idea that is important in our daily lives—remembering how to spell it and pronounce it, and then worrying about what my friends would think if I were to use it in normal conversation, are reasons enough to remove it from serious consideration.

Certainly we realize that our use of words marks us in a number of ways. Sociolinguists identify certain words, for example, as *socio-economic markers*. That is, our use or avoidance of these words identifies us with a specific social class and a particular economic category. To make matters worse, socio-economic markers can vary from one part of the country to another; regional dialects dictate the status of words. If you live in southern Illinois, you probably pronounce the word *creek* differently, depending upon whether you are educated, middle class, and middle income, or uneducated, lower class, and lower income. If you are the latter, you probably pronounce the word as *crick*. However, if you live in Wisconsin, the word *creek* is not a socio-economic marker and you are likely to pronounce the word as *crick*, regardless of your socio-economic status.

Although we may know *why* people use certain words, we do not know for certain *how they learn* the words they use. Most children learn over 5,000 words, to which they have immediate and easy access by the time they enter the first grade. We assume that children have learned most of these words without the benefit of any kind of formal instruction, direct or indirect!

In addition, we have different ways of counting the words that people know, depending upon what we mean by *know* and why we are counting the words. Certainly, vocabulary is determined to a large extent by the purposes and functions we have for words in our language. The same is true for reading teachers and other reading educators. To determine how best to teach vocabulary, we must first determine the purposes and functions that the vocabulary is to serve.

VOCABULARY: ITS FUNCTIONS AND PURPOSES

Some of the difficulty with knowing words is that *to know* can mean a variety of things. If we think of the four primary language-producing and language-consuming domains of speaking, writing, reading, and listening, we immediately note an obvious division of the senses of *know* for vocabulary. Our language-producing vocabulary—speaking and writing—is substantively smaller than our listening and reading vocabularies. Some estimates, in fact, place the difference between these two as being twice as many words in our reading and listening group. Although this estimate might not be precise, it is certainly true that we need to have considerably more ownership of our *production* vocabularies than our more general *employment* categories.

Although the reasons for this difference vary, a dominant one is probably that our daily lives do not require us to produce many of the words in our production vocabulary. We can relegate *cacophony* to our reading vocabulary; i.e., we know what the most likely literal and possibly figurative uses of the word are in print or oral discourse. Since for most of us using the words in speech would be neither comfortable nor appropriate, having it in our reading and listening vocabularies is ample. In other words, *cacophony* is a word that is likely to show up in our reading and might appear in our listening vocabulary, if we are in professions where it is either an appropriate technical term (for instance, music or accoustically related fields) or a term that would be used figuratively in formal address.

Unfortunately, simply saying that *cacophony* is in our reading vocabulary is not enough to indicate what degree of ownership we have of the word. For instance, there are many words in our reading vocabulary that we could easily transfer into our production vocabularies. On the other hand, there are some words in our reading vocabulary which have tenuous status at best. That is, with a little luck, a good deal of contextual assistance, and some related prior experience or background knowledge, we can get a fix on the word and appropriate enough meaning to it to make it textually functional in a given passage. And, of course, between these two extremes within our reading vocabulary, there are a number of vocabularies for which we have degrees of ownership.

In other words, although there is obvious overlap, our reading and listening vocabularies are more extensive than are our speaking and writing vocabularies. The additional words in our reading and listening vocabularies reflect various degrees of ownership, from nearly as complete as those in our production vocabularies to extremely tenuous, accessible only with effort and, sometimes, luck.

For ease of discussion, let's divide the reading vocabulary range into three categories of words, or dictionaries*—the ownership dictionary; the mid-level dictionary (accessible with contextual assistance); and the low-level dictionary (marginal; possible, but with increased risk of error). We can depict these graphically as follows:

Each of us possesses all three dictionaries in our heads. We can make entries into any of these dictionaries when we experience a new word in our language environment. This may occur through reading, or we may hear it in any of a variety of contexts.

Normally, initial entry is made into the mid-level or low-level dictionaries. Transfer may eventually be effected from the lower-level dictionaries to the ownership dictionary, although in special contexts or in unique situations, it is possible to move a new word directly into our ownership dictionary. However, these contexts and situations are not commonplace, and most entries are made into the lower-level dictionaries.

The matter is further complicated somewhat in that new entries can be made as *low-level* entries, as *mid-level* entries, or as *high-level* entries into any of the dictionaries. For example:

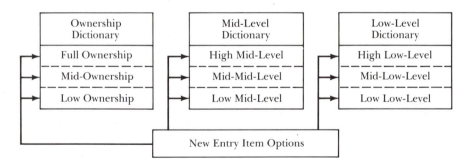

The same is true generally for low-level and mid-level dictionary transfers. Vocabulary in either of these dictionaries can be transferred to a higher-level dictionary with the entry at any level in the new dictionary. Normally,

---

*We shall use *dictionary* in the linguistic sense of being the total vocabulary in a given access range that exists in our heads. In this chapter, we shall talk about three dictionaries in our heads that are important for reading vocabulary and comprehension instruction.

however, the transfer comes from high levels in one dictionary to a lower level in the higher-level dictionary. For example:

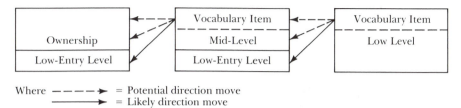

Where ---- ➤ = Potential direction move
———➤ = Likely direction move

Although our dictionaries grow over the years as a result of experience and instruction, the three dictionary categories do not. Our full ownership category increases in volume—we hope—as we transfer dictionary entries to it from our mid-level dictionary, accessible with assistance. Remember, however, that new vocabulary items being are normally entered into either one of two dictionaries, the mid-level dictionary or the low-level dictionary.

Some of our reading vocabulary instruction is intended to introduce new vocabulary to the low-level dictionary. Most direct instruction is usually intended to result in vocabulary items being entered directly into the mid-level dictionary, assuming that the instruction is relevant, appropriate, and effective. Some of it enters only the low-level dictionary, and some, of course, enters no dictionary.

Thus arises the question of reading vocabulary instruction and its effectiveness generally. One of the difficulties in determining the kind of instruction we use and deciding upon its effectiveness is that the question presumes a previous determination of which dictionary we are aiming at. There are good reasons for assuming that different instructional models are appropriate for different reading vocabulary dictionaries.

As a general rule, when we consider the difference between those models of reading vocabulary instruction that are direct and specific to particular entries and those models that, the research suggests, derive from a rich literacy environment (where both classroom material resources and the richness of the language used for functional and motivated purposes abound), the former is usually directed toward the mid-level dictionary, the latter toward the low-level dictionary. There obviously are many exceptions to this general rule.

Of major importance, however, is the fact that the reading teacher, intent upon improving reading vocabulary, must determine **prior to instruction** the purpose for the instruction and the function or functions that the new dictionary entries will serve.

As worthwhile as it sounds initially, it is not necessarily important for students eventually to have full ownership of all the words we teach them. However, once an entry is made into a dictionary, even at the low level, it gradually works its way up through the higher-level dictionaries. Many, in fact, will even transfer out of the reading vocabulary dictionaries and into the language-producing dictionaries, i.e., speaking and writing. As a general rule and regardless of strategy or technique, direct reading vocabulary instruction tends to aim at the *access dictionary* (the mid-level dictionary). When evaluating instructional effectiveness then, we must be careful *not* to assume that the full ownership dictionary is the goal.

Many of the direct-instruction models included in basal readers, spelling books, and other commercially developed vocabulary-building materials tacitly suggest that they are designed to teach to full-ownership dictionaries. For example, most will ask students to pronounce a new word, state a definition for the word orally or in writing or both, and use the word in a sentence, orally or in writing or both. In these instances, the requirement that the student *use* the word in a meaningful statement in one or both of the language-producing modes implies that the instruction will help the student make the entry into the top-level dictionary; in fact, the brevity of the instruction, coupled with its likely separation from use of the word on a daily basis in both speaking and writing, practically assures that such a top-level entry cannot be made.

In addition and of major significance is the fact that regardless of the instructional model or models that we use to teach reading vocabulary, these models should contribute either directly or indirectly to the students' developing strategies of vocabulary acquisition and use. We want students **to learn how to learn new reading vocabulary**; to develop their own strategies for building and expanding their personal dictionaries and for moving entries from one dictionary to another. Otherwise, their reading vocabulary growth will be extremely limited. As teachers of reading vocabulary, it is our primary responsibility to see that the actual new vocabulary children learn *under* our tutelage is miniscule compared to what they will learn *because* of our tutelage!

What Students Must Know

For the learner to enter any new words into one of his or her dictionaries, he or she must know the basics of language structure and how it functions. During the primary grades, selected new vocabulary, or *sight words*, are taught directly with virtually no attempt to analyze them either structurally or semantically. New vocabulary tends to be the common words necessary to bind the language together, those that the beginning reader must have for the initial stages of formal reading instruction; these words are often difficult to define or analyze structurally, e.g., articles such as *a, an,* and *the* or prepositions such as *of, in, out,* and so on.

We shall not go into the pros and cons of sight-word instruction and its strategies. However, it seems reasonable to assert that such expectations in early reading instruction are proper and necessary. Instruction seems relatively painless, and young students get enough dictionary entries to enable them to read quickly.

Other than the early sight-word instruction, additional acquisition of vocabulary during classroom instruction requires learners to apply skills in four different areas.

Phonics

We assume that students know how to phonologically segment words when they learn new vocabulary in other than sight-word contexts. Being able to sound out a word with a reasonable approximation of its correct pronunciation is an important step in being comfortable with the process of new-word acquisition, if nothing else.

Since phonics skills are acquired early enough in reading programs, other means of direct instruction in reading vocabulary can take place. Remember, however, that children can have decoding skill difficulties well beyond the first grade; some learners never develop the necessary phonological analysis and application skills requisite for major new reading vocabulary acquisition. If that is the case, the other four skill application areas become mainly inaccessible to them.

Structural Analysis

To use instructional models based upon the student's ability to structurally analyze words, the teacher must assume that the student has some degree of morphological (word formation) knowledge and, further, an ability to morphologically analyze words. Students need to know the difference between free morphemes—main meaning-bearing units from which words are built and exemplified by single-syllable words, e.g., *law*—and bound morphemes—the secondary meaning-bearing units in longer words, e.g., prefixes and suffixes. For example, the word *unlawful* is made up of the free morpheme *law* and the two bound morphemes *un* and *ful*, the former a prefix, the latter a suffix.

The teacher must also assume that students know the meanings of root words, prefixes, and suffixes, and the different roles played by inflectional and derivational endings of words, i.e., plural, possessive, tense, and descriptor form indicators.

Instruction designed to teach students the phonological and morphological character of the language, and the necessary skills associated with using this knowledge to acquire new reading vocabulary rightfully belongs in a category of instruction better thought of as being *pre-new reading vocabulary* in nature.

The remaining two skill categories tend to overlap more significantly with actual instruction in new reading vocabulary, although they too can be thought of as being pre-new reading vocabulary.

Contextual Analysis

The ability to use various contextual clues to determine a word's meaning is probably the single most important ability a developing reader can have. Throughout our lives we enter most new vocabulary into our mid-level dictionary or low-level dictionary. These entries are acquired either by applying context clues in our reading or, in a more limited application, by using outside references such as a desk dictionary.

Although certain basic contextual application skills are acquired fairly early in the reading program and used in building new vocabulary, more sophisticated and subtle uses of context clues require direct instruction and more experience with a wider variety of texts and text types.

Supplemental Reference

Although the desk dictionary and thesaurus are the most direct sources of new words, most of us, including those with the necessary knowledge and skills, do not bother to use these tools. Therefore, we need to teach students how to use these tools and to develop a positive attitude toward their habitual use during reading.

Remember, although we prefer to think that all four of these skill categories are pre-conditions to both direct and indirect instruction in reading vocabulary, we may reasonably assume that many of our students will not have mastered all of the phonics and structural analysis skills, even in the later grades. Further, note that contextual analysis skills and supplemental reference skills, even if developed in basics, should become increasingly sophisticated and refined through the grades. Teaching techniques and activities that incorporate instruction in the use of the desk dictionary and thesaurus legitimately fall within the domain of those approaches designed to help students develop the necessary metacognitive facilities for ongoing reading vocabulary acquisition and use.

The Appropriate Dictionary

As we said earlier, before instruction in reading vocabulary begins, the teacher must decide what the purpose or function of the new vocabulary will be. Are we striving for full-ownership dictionary status or will low-level entry do? In social studies, if we are starting a new chapter on economic policies that shaped the economic development of much of the world and my students will meet the new word *mercantilism*, then I want at least mid-level dictionary status, but preferably full-ownership status. If, in English, my students will be reading *David Copperfield* and I know that one of Dickens's favorite words in that novel is *pecuniary*, I probably will be satisfied with mid-level dictionary status (although this entry level is not sufficient, since the word is tied so closely to the theme and tone of the work). In science, if the word *specious* appears in an article my students will be reading in the next assignment, and it is a new word for them, I suspect low-level dictionary entry might be sufficient (with context clues and knowledge of language structure generally adequate for the task, provided I do some direct instruction).

In the latter case, if the word goes into the low-level dictionary, its status will likely remain stable until need dictates its transfer to the mid-level dictionary. Although the word *specious* is not critical to comprehension of other science concepts, its importance, like that of many other words, is strictly tied to its contribution to overall knowledge (an important domain that makes use of the continually expanding entry levels in our various dictionaries). The new entries in the low-level dictionary battle each other for transfer into the mid-level dictionary. Again, literacy demands in our daily affairs determine the winners and the losers.

As a general rule of thumb, the following guidelines can be helpful for determining the kind of instruction I need based upon new vocabulary functions.

1. New reading vocabulary that is critical to comprehension of major concepts or ideas central to subject matter, and which we want our students to be able to apply in a variety of text modes, deserves concentrated, direct formal instruction and direct informal instruction. Further, ongoing practice and application demands must be made on the students so that they internalize both the processes of the acquisition and the ability to apply the new word in a variety of contexts and for a variety of purposes. In short, we want the word entered into the ownership dictionary as soon as possible.

In the early grades, we are tempted to include too many new vocabulary items in this category, because we can think of so many words that second and third graders do not yet possess but which most people use on a common basis. However, if we are realistic about our time limitations and the developmental stage of our learners, and further, if we recognize the powerful role played by children's experiences in a rich literacy environment (where they are surrounded by books, magazines, newspapers, the positive and addictive habits of literacy involvement), then we can aim much of this new vocabulary instruction at the low-level and mid-level dictionaries.

2. New words that recur in the various forms of text our students read—words which are not crucial to comprehension of the thesis or central theme but do contribute to its overall meaning—are important enough for entry into the mid-level dictionary. These are *enabling* words; they open doors to new knowledge if we can consciously apply them in new reading contexts.

Many of the instructional techniques and strategies for teaching new reading vocabulary for mid-level dictionary entry may do so by helping us achieve minimum entry requirements. That is, they provide enough word knowledge for the learner to make the entry but not enough for consistent use of the word in different reading contexts. For example, teaching reading vocabulary by using analogies is one means some teachers use to gain dictionary entry status for selected new words. Although such instruction often achieves that goal, the instruction falls short of moving the word to the top of the mid-level dictionary, where most words appear that are ready or nearly ready for transfer to the ownership dictionary. Other direct instruction models are probably more appropriate for the latter goal.

3. Within the three dictionaries, there are additional ranges of priority which the learner places on individual entries. Since the dictionaries constantly shuffle entries around within themselves as well as move entries from one to another, entry status in any given dictionary is dictated not only by the desires or goals of the teacher but also by the *need* of the learner. The greater the learner feels the need for individual new words, the more likely he or she will give the new word an elevated status in whatever dictionary it enters.

4. Finally, and probably most important, is that the purposes and goals of the instruction in reading vocabulary, the desires of the teacher, and the need imposed by the learner all work to create a *"zone of proximal development."* The zone of proximal development was conceptualized many years ago by noted Russian developmental psychologist Lev Vygotsky. Vygotsky, studying the development of thought and language in children in the 1920s and early 1930s, noted (as did Piaget) that children move developmentally through cognitive stages, i.e., preoperational stages to concrete operations to the stage of formal reasoning. However, the movement is subtle. Children do not go to bed one night in the preoperational stage and awake the next morning in the stage of concrete operations! There are transition periods between stages and within stages for specific cognitive facilities. Vygotsky posited that the most lucrative instructional time was during this transition period for individual children (Vygotsky, 1962).

We can apply Vygotksy's concept analagously to the acquisition and employment of reading vocabulary. Words already entered in one of the dictionaries jockey for positions of power, as was noted earlier. At any given time a number of words are ready to move from one dictionary to another, and unknown words are more susceptible to instruction for entry into one of the lower-level dictionaries.

Given this condition, teachers need to do the following: (a) Know individual students and their language. Has Billy been using a new word in his writing or speaking? Have you noticed that Meredith obviously assimilated a new word in her oral reading the other day? And what about John?

Do you recall how he made a miscue with a new word in his reading the other day? He still doesn't have the word *influence* in a dictionary yet, but with a little push, it will easily go into an entry-level status in the low- or mid-level dictionary. (b) Include teaching techniques and activities designed to help students move dictionary entries from a lower level to a higher one within the dictionary and, further, to move individual entries from one dictionary to a higher one, e.g., from mid-level dictionary to ownership dictionary.

It is clear that reading vocabulary instruction in a comprehensive program should encompass more than simply developing teaching techniques, strategies, and activities for the addition of new words. Instruction should also be aimed very directly at capitalizing upon students' zones of proximal development as prime opportunities for either moving dictionary entries about or adding new ones.

READING VOCABULARY MODELS

From our earlier discussion, we can easily imagine how difficult it is to decide which teaching strategies, techniques, and activities are best to achieve the desired dictionary placement. That is, you may choose a particular teaching technique because it is appropriate for a particular text. Some techniques and activities do seem to work better with some texts and text types. Or, you may choose an activity because you haven't used it for awhile and you want some variety. There are many other reasons for doing it one way today and another way tomorrow, most of which are probably legitimate.

In addition, we must remember the individual ability range in our class as well as the current vocabulary each student has to work with. For grades four through twelve, Smith (1941) estimated a 6,000-word gap between a child at the twenty-fifth percentile in vocabulary and a child at the fiftieth percentile. Nagy and Herman (1985) estimate that the reading vocabulary of the average child grows at a rate of about 3,000 words a year between grades three and twelve. It is reasonable to estimate that the difference in vocabulary growth per year through these grades could be at least 1,000 words, while the difference in vocabulary acquisition between low and high achievers would be even greater.

Therefore, it is impossible, for example, to categorize a teaching technique or activity designed for the whole class that would achieve mid-level dictionary entry for all the students. Many would already have full ownership, others would probably not even have low-level dictionary status after the lesson, much less before. However, we can make some general observations about possible relationships between specific strategies, techniques, and activities.

The DFI, DII, and III Models

Direct formal instruction (DFI) models for reading vocabulary, when used in conjunction with a long-range strategy for keeping the new words up-front in the most likely functional-use contexts, and when used in conjunction with a rich language-use, literacy-involved environment, possess the highest degree of likelihood of bringing totally new words directly into the ownership dictionary of the learner. Further, they most certainly have the best chance of moving existing dictionary entries into higher-level dictionaries, including the ownership dictionary.

Direct informal instruction (DII) models have the capacity to move mid-level dictionary entries into the ownership dictionary, to move entries within the mid-level dictionary from lower to higher status, and to move new low-level entries into the mid-level dictionary.

DII models, however, generally lack necessary power—even when accompanied by other positive attributes such as rich, language-use classroom environments—for the development of full-ownership status for entries previously unknown to the user. However, they have tremendous power for helping learners make fairly quick entry shifts. This is particularly true when they are used at times when students are in zones of proximal development for the words being taught.

Indirect informal instruction (III) models have as their primary goals long-range reading vocabulary development, reinforcement for existing dictionaries, and the development of motivation for new entries or moving existing entries to higher status. These models should be an ongoing part of all language arts/reading classes and used in a variety of contexts where the other models are inappropriate either because of the subject at hand or because of the time limitations.

We shall categorize strategies, techniques, and activities by the above three types. However, it must be remembered that conditions such as prior knowledge can determine the cognitive level at which a student functions and the likely success of a given vocabulary instruction strategy or technique. We are establishing the three categories to give the teacher a rational scheme for designing his or her approach to reading vocabulary instruction.

The following additional guidelines should help teachers when planning to use the three models in reading vocabulary instruction:

1. Select teaching approaches from all three models.
2. Carefully note differences between strategies, techniques, and activities.
3. Tie reading vocabulary instruction to *all* classes and to *all* subject areas. Student sense of need determines the effectiveness of any and all instruction. Motivation is likely to be greater when the functional uses of reading vocabulary is related to ideas or content of interest and purpose to the learner.
4. Select your approach in terms of your purposes and goals and in terms of the three dictionaries students are working with and where you want entries to be made or shifted to or from.

5. Try to be tuned-in at all times to the vocabularies of individual students so that you may more logically estimate when the zone of proximal development is present for each and precisely where that zone is.

6. At all times **emphasize that learning and using new words is fun!**

DFI Models

Most strategies for teaching reading vocabulary can be categorized as DFI models. Because these models do not yield to change and are not subject to inconsistency (two important attributes of a teaching strategy), they are most likely to be used over time in an ongoing and consistent manner. Although they may be used in any or all of the three reading phases, because of their nature, they tend to be used more often in the prereading phase.

In addition, a number of different techniques and activities can be used to support DFI strategies. These should reflect creativity and variety; in some instances at least, a little unpredictability adds spice and interest to the instruction.

However, with DFI models, the patterned and predictable consistency enables the teacher to structure a scope and sequence of reading vocabulary and vocabulary types for instruction throughout the year, and for the district to make plans for the full grade spectrum. Further, the DFI models are necessary components of the reading program if there is to be the most effective possible growth in this area (Anderson and Freebody, 1977; Beck and McKeown, 1985; and others).

Although reading authorities do not all agree on what the best DFI models are—in fact, they very often disagree—most see the need for *some* direct instruction in the reading program. Further, most proposed models reflect our requirements that a model be a teaching strategy rather than a technique or activity. Following are two examples of useful strategies for developing reading vocabularies.

A Five-Step Model for DFI

This strategy works most effectively for teaching selection vocabulary during the prereading phase.

1. Look at the word. Say the word. The word can be presented to students in a variety of ways. It may be viewed directly in the text, or the teacher can write it on the board or on an overhead projector transparency. At least most of the time the word should be presented in the context of a sentence, and this sentence should be dominated by vocabulary in the students' dictionaries. The word should be highlighted (e.g., underlining, boldface, italics). Be sure that all students can pronounce the word correctly before moving on to Step two. If there are questions about why it is pronounced as it is, take some time to discuss the reasons. Step three will go into this area in greater detail. The primary and only concern at this first step is that the students be able to pronounce the word correctly, even if that means simply modeling your pronunciation of it.

To vary this first step, use an inductive technique with related activities. For example, present a sequence of words with similar spelling and structural characteristics. Point out to the students that the meanings of these words (which they already know how to pronounce) are not important. However, they should look at the words' similarities in sound to give them a clue as to how the new word is pronounced.

The decision to use an inductive technique in this first step is determined by a couple of factors. One factor is the dictionary in which you want most of your students to make the entry. Normally, you will find that time on task is closely correlated with knowledge acquired. An inductive technique requires more class time, means more discussion and opportunity for new word use, and generally involves the learner to a greater extent. Another related factor is the importance of the new word to the reading of the text. Significance in text to be read determines in large measure the importance of the vocabulary item for dictionary entry and, thus, the amount of time you will commit to the instruction.

Remember that although the strategy should remain consistent and predictable, we should also strive for some variety in techniques and activities to keep motivation and interest high. That means that, in some instances at least, you will want to mix inductive approaches with deductive techniques (where you simply present the information directly to the students).

2. Tell the meaning of the word.   Provide a definition of the word that is most appropriate to the meaning or meanings used in the text. This is normally not the time to present alternative definitions unless such definitions are important to the comprehension of this particular text. Remember, too, that secondary definitions are more easily acquired through techniques and activities in DII and III models.

Again, as in Step one, you may choose to use either inductive or deductive techniques. You might provide students with a brief list of synonyms and ask them to infer a meaning for the new word. Or, you might provide them with semantic clues and ask them to predict the word meaning. Directly stating the meaning yourself is a straightforward deductive method of presenting the word. Remember to use both speaking and writing, whichever technique you choose to go with.

Also, take advantage of this step to use the desk dictionary as a resource tool. Vary your techniques so that sometimes you look the word up, sometimes your students do.

3. Analyze the word structurally. This third step is where you do a detailed structural analysis of the word. Identify the root word or base morpheme along with prefix or suffix. Separate the components in writing on the board or overhead. Discuss the meanings of each morpheme in the word. (You might have to do some homework on the generic meanings of some prefixes and suffixes prior to the lesson).

Ask students for related words that have the same structural characteristics or features. For example, what are some words that begin with the same prefix or end with the same suffix? How are their meanings similar because of that structural similarity? Can they find words in their text that are structurally similar?

4. Discuss the word. The fourth step of this DFI model allows the greatest flexibility in the strategy. The teacher must determine here the amount of time warranted, observe carefully where each student is, i.e., look for performance indicators of dictionary entry in students, and adjust teaching techniques and activities accordingly.

This step is critical; here the students brings together structural, semantic, and contextual information to determine the role of the word in his or her life and, therefore, dictionary entry status!

Normally, you want to present other examples of the word in use, point out synonyms, antonyms, homophones, and homographs, if they are of interest or worthy of note. Again, you must decide how much time to commit to this and determine the role or roles of various inductive and deductive techniques and activities.

5. Use the word in context. The last step of this strategy places function and language context front and center. Although there are opportunities for using sentence context throughout the previous steps, in this final step context becomes even more important. Have available a number of different sentence contexts from different texts where the word is used. Be sure *not* to use examples where different senses of the word are employed; i.e., you want the word to mean the same as it does in the text the student is reading. However, it is important to demonstrate the word's versatility and usefulness in different reading contexts.

Have students make up sentences—orally and in writing—using the word appropriately. Ask them to exchange papers with a friend and assess each other's use of the word. Discuss the sentences in class.

Variations of this model can work effectively also. Remember, however, to keep the steps consistent and orderly. We want our students **to predict** what the next step will be and **to develop** a personal strategy similar in character to this one as they approach new words in their reading.

A Topic-Centered Model for DFI

A topic-centered DFI model is a strategy that also has a series of steps. However, there are a number of significant differences beyond that similarity. To begin with, this strategy extends beyond a single lesson. It is designed for one week or more of work in a specific unit that has a central theme or topic. It works well in language arts/reading classes and also in classes such as science, social studies, math, and others—in fact, it is applicable in any situation where there is a central theme or topic in the instructional unit. The steps of the strategy follow.

1. Choose a theme. You must choose a theme, topic, or thesis central to the text content for a specific period of time beyond a single lesson, e.g., a one-week unit. This might mean clustering stories or poetry for a unit that is theme dominated, e.g. focusing a social studies unit on "Following the Yellow Brick Road" (about the need of individuals to pursue new directions in search of themselves or others). This is a relatively easy way to organize content for instruction since so many basal readers, social studies textbooks, literature series, and science books are already designed in this fashion.

Prepare students for the unit by employing a range of activities designed to activate prior knowledge or to build their background knowledge. The need to provide ample motivation goes without saying.

2. Select theme-related words. After identifying a term or phrase which defines the unit's theme, identify a group of new words that is related closely to the theme and that is important to the text. Generally, you should view the theme-identifier word or phrase as a category label broad enough to encompass the related new vocabulary to be taught. A thesaurus and dictionary are valuable tools here. However, the words you choose should not be synonyms so much as *collocates* of the identifier word. (The term *collocate* is one used by anthropologists and sociolinguists to identify the sort of semantic magnetism that most words that are labels have.) For example, if I told you that we would be reading a text about a trip to a farm pond, you might anticipate that a number of words would likely appear in that text; the word *pond* attracts to it collocates such as *water, mud, weeds, rippling, cattails, fish, turtle, snake, sand, clear,* and so on. If we think of the theme of *Law,* what are some collocates likely to be attracted? Of course they include words such as *justice, court, judge, trial, jury,* and so on.

Keep the list of new words brief but relative to the length of the unit. Obviously, the longer the unit, the greater the number of new words you can introduce. As a general rule, three to five words per day for grades four through twelve is reasonable. Adjust downward for the primary grades, and upward as appropriate to content and ability of learners.

3. Introduce theme-related words.   Introduce the words to your students in context and ask them to guess the possible meanings from contextual clues. Provide amply opportunity for students to discuss the word and its meaning and use the word in a meaningful context. Dictionary and thesaurus uses are excellent during this step of the strategy. Include in your discussions ample reference to the role the word will play in the unit you are studying.

Remember that since this is an extended teaching unit, time devoted to new vocabulary carefully chosen can be critical to the success or failure of the unit. Therefore, when you consider time spent, do not forget that fact.

4. Go beyond the text and classroom.   This is especially important since the unit is extended over time; the opportunities to capitalize upon that time require that you look to sources and experiences away from direct instruction and the text. The following possibilities are excellent options:

- Have your students keep notebooks during the unit's duration. Ask them to record incidents of the new words used at home, on the playground, in other settings, and in other reading. Ask them to document their observations and include a brief description of where, when, and how each observation took place. You can have team or paired contests to see who can come up with the most documented cases of use. This works particularly well with younger students. Daily discussion of notebook entries is important. This will require considerable effort and commitment from your students, so you should make every effort to assure them that you value this activity.
- Make thesaurus and dictionary assignments or have classroom activities (games, contests, and so on) using these tools.
- Have students do *word etymology searches*. Word etymology or word history searches tied to the unit's theme can be excellent activities for students to engage in outside of class. (There will be more on word etymology techniques and activities later in this chapter.)

5. Review all words at the end of the unit.   Remember it is important to periodically review all study for reading vocabulary. Since this unit extends beyond a single lesson, and some time may have passed since earlier new words were taught, it is essential to review. If the unit is fairly long, you must have more frequent reviews followed by a summary review of all words at the close of the unit.

Include writing and oral language-use activities as part of the end-of-unit review. Again, the length of the review should be commensurate with or proportionate to the length and importance of the unit.

6. Practice maintaining new vocabulary.   The primary purpose of a DFI reading strategy is to assure the highest possible dictionary entry level for the new words. To do this, continued use in appropriate contexts and for appropriate purposes provides the greatest assurance of dictionary entry for students. Therefore, the teacher must attempt to keep the words in frequent use—in classroom discussion, in writing assignments, in future reading assignments, and in whatever other ways are available.

DII Models

The DII models are primarily designed to enhance DFI strategies *and* to provide the learner with additional help in moving dictionary entries from a lower to a higher dictionary or, to a more limited extent, to introduce new entries. The models presented in this section are both schema based and text based. Although not exhaustive in quantity, they represent a fairly comprehensive range of types that lend themselves to formal instruction.

As you read through these techniques and activities, you will discover that with appropriate modification most of these examples can be used across a wide range of grades and with a wide range of student ability. Clearly, some are more satisfactory for upper grades than they are for earlier grades.

Using Context Clues

Most avid readers depend upon contextual assistance for generating meaning for new words. In fact, most of us do not bother to rely on a dictionary, even when we should; we are confident enough in our reading abilities to assume that we can understand the author's use of a new word from information in the text and from ourselves.

Context clues come in a variety of forms and ways. Some, within sentences, are structural or grammatical in character. For example, definition by apposition in text is sometimes used: "A gofer, one who runs errands for the team in a chili contest, is entertaining as well as being functional in other worthwhile ways."

Definition by apposition is also cued by use of the semicolon, especially when the concept being defined is more abstract or complex. Here, the semicolon typically separates complete clauses rather than single words or short phrases. For example, "All important general labeling words attract collocates; a collection of like terms which are attracted to the general labeling term, usually through semantic rather than grammatical associations."

Although it is certainly important that students learn how to use statements of apposition, of synonym and antonym, of definition by operation or example, and semicolon cues to generate meaning for new words, these are probably not the most important or even most common of the context clues that efficient readers use during the reading act.

Consider the following for example:

Psychological quietism, besides justifying the profit motive and providing an explanation of unemployment and the aversion to disagreeable employment which exculpates prevailing economic institutions, has served a third purpose. It was once widely used and is still invoked to argue against an adequate program of social security.

H. Girvetz, *The Evolution of Liberalism,*

Consider the predictions we can make from the context of this passage (the possibility that the passage might be taken out of context notwithstanding):

1. *Psychological quietism* probably is some sort of condition or attribute of a given economic policy or doctrine. The base word of *quiet* in the phrase implies that psychological quietism is some kind of a hands-off policy; let institutions or the market determine profit (and so on).

2. The author is probably a liberal in both politics and economics. Psychological quietism would be an attribute of more conservative policies in both areas. And, the author is clearly in opposition to psychological quietism. The first statement clearly associates *profit motive* with the beliefs and behaviors of those not sensitive to larger social needs. The use of the term *adequate* in the last statement suggests that psychological quietism, a policy the author does not like, works against the social security system.

3. *Exculpates* is a word I've seen before in my reading, but my grasp of it is marginal. It must be in my low-level dictionary, because I'm willing to predict that it means something like "supports or gives comfort to." (Actually it means "frees from responsibility or guilt," so my prediction is close enough, although not right on target.)

4. The author talks about psychological quietism lending credence to a concept of *disagreeable employment*. I haven't heard of that as I can recall, but since it is associated with economic policies the author is opposed to, he or she apparently wants me to respond negatively to the concept. This is easy for most readers, since those of us who are working can't think of much that is negative about employment, if we need work badly enough.

Or, consider a somewhat simpler but quite similar passage:

JoAnn was not looking forward to her first day at Western Washington University. She had spent most of her school-year life in fine private boarding schools in the East, except for summer travels to Europe with her parents. Fine clothes, expensive cars, fine food in the best restaurants, that had been her life. Why do mom and dad want her to go to college here anyway? And live in a dorm? Have a roommate? How thoroughly disgusting and *provincial!* This was going to be a completely *debilitating* year! Now, at least her roommate, Beth, was ready for dinner and suggested they go out to McDonald's. JoAnn thought, "I've never heard of it, but it sounds quite elegant. Ah, for some superb *cuisine*, finally! Think I'll start with *vichyssoise*, then move on to my *entree* of . . . ."

Now for some predictions from this text:

1. In this excerpt, the author wants to show how difficult it could be for an individual reared in a protected, wealthy environment, with the best of everything, to relate to the world that most of us live in.

2. Both *provincial* and *debilitating* must be negative terms because JoAnn associates them with bad things or things she doesn't like. They probably aren't that bad to everybody though, because JoAnn sounds very spoiled. *Provincial* must have something to do with common people and what they do. *Debilitated* must mean that she's going to feel badly, or she's not going to like what life is like for the year.

3. *Cuisine* must mean good food, like that served in expensive restaurants, because that's what JoAnn is used to and it's the first time in the text that she is enthused about anything.

4. I still don't know what *vichyssoise* means, except that it is something like an appetizer eaten before the main meal. That's what the *entree* is because I've seen that on menus in restaurants that we go to, even if they don't have *cuisine*!

In each of the above examples, notice how the reader uses both structural and content clues found directly in the text, *and* personal background knowledge and prior experience to make predictions about the new vocabulary appearing in each.

In our first excerpt, the author's tone or mood was central to our use of context clues. We locked onto the tone and made our decisions from context clues based upon that tone and what we thought the author's point of view was. To some extent, the same is true in the latter text, where the author's point of view also affected our responses. However, here we were influenced by the major contrast that existed between the two different worlds of our main character.

In both cases, we brought to bear as much as we could from our background knowledge about economics and food on the one hand, and about our knowledge of the world in general and what people believe and do in that world on the other.

This is what effective reading is about—using contextual assistance provided by (a) the text, its structure, and content, and (b) background knowledge and prior experience to impose meanings on unfamiliar words.

The techniques and activities that follow are intended to tap both of the critical contextual assistance areas—the text and the reader.

Fortunately (unfortunately?), while I was working on this chapter of the book, my stepdaughter insisted upon reading to me particularly fascinating articles from the newspaper. The first had to do with arguments people use when they have been stopped for speeding. The reporter had interviewed a police officer, who offered several examples. Among them was the observation that "I was speeding because I thought my plant was moribund." I asked Meredith what she thought *moribund* meant. She said she did not know. She read on, "She told the officer that the plant did not look well, was very dry, the leaves were wilted, and it *was* very expensive. She was afraid it was probably moribund. I asked Meredith again what the term *moribund* meant. She responded that "it was something that was either very sick or dead!" In fact, she was correct. Although this is neither a normal context nor a normal use of the term, the somewhat extended textual assistance allowed her to make a reasonably accurate projection about the normal meanings associated with the term.

Later the same morning, she read another article about "people who clustered about the parameter of an event." I asked her what she thought the term *parameter* meant. She responded, quickly, without studying the text again, that "*parameters* were the fences or boundaries around something"—not bad, if not right, for a teenager, I thought. *Parameter* and *perimeter*, in fact, are often used interchangeably if incorrectly. I told her to read it one more time, thinking about the idea in general and about the words around *parameter* in particular. She did and stated that *parameter* had "something to do with the most important part, or something like that"—a reasonably accurate paraphrase of the normal definition of *parameter* as "a measure of central tendency or determination around which related or supporting data cluster."

This anecdote demonstrates quite graphically an important point about contextual assistance. It is not only the amount of background knowledge and prior experience readers have which determines their ability to use contextual clues, but also the amount of information provided by the text which determines readers' ability to generate meaning for unknown words.

The techniques and activities which follow vary in the amount of textual assistance they provide. Remember that modification of the content of these examples can be done to increase or decrease textual assistance as desired or needed.

Using Nonce Words

Provide students with brief paragraphs that use a nonsense word. Ask them to use the surrounding information and what they know about the subject to write a definition for the term. For example:

John felt *scarfly* this afternoon. Things had not gone well all day. School had been a drag. He had an argument with one of his best friends. And now his mom was on to him for leaving his room a mess. *Scarfly!* That's how he felt."

Scarfly means:

_____

Or,

Jean saw the most *jemptious* new sweater at the Washington Square Mall. It was loose knit and sort of a mauve color with baggy arms and V-neck. She felt she just had to have it.

Jemptious means:

_____

This activity can be made easier or more challenging by varying the number of useful cues, or by choosing more difficult or abstract themes or topics.

Follow this activity with assignments for your students to write similar paragraphs using nonce word; in some instances you can provide the words, in others have them make up their own words. Have the students then exchange these paragraphs with classmates and try to predict reasonable definitions for the nonce words.

Remember to capitalize upon the discussion opportunities that this activity provides. Ask students to tell how they figured out the meaning of the word, what specific clues in the text helped them, what they knew before the reading that they could bring to the text to determine a reasonable meaning, and so on. Since this activity is based primarily on handouts or worksheets, it is too easy to let students work individually without the useful and important sharing and discussing that gives it power. Fight that temptation! Keep oral language and writing front and center.

Using the Cloze

The cloze was developed several years ago initially as a means to assess the readability of materials. It fairly quickly got shifted into use as an informal assessment device to test readers' comprehension of text. A less common use, but one that is perhaps more appropriate than any other for the cloze, is instructional.

To cloze a passage of text you simply delete every nth word or, in the case of instructional uses, selected words, and replace the word with a 15-space blank.* Ask students to write in the appropriate words.

_____

*When the cloze is used as an informal reading comprehension assessment device, the rules for use are quite fixed: (1) Select a text passage of at least 50 words. (2) Delete every fifth word, with the first deletion chosen at random from words one through eleven. (3) Replace each deleted word with a fifteen-space blank line. (4) Ask students to fill in each blank with the *exact* missing word after you have given them basic background information on what the passage is excerpted from, what it is about generally, and so on.

Students who choose the correct word for at least one third of the blanks are said to be reading with adequate comprehension for guided instruction. Students who choose the correct word for at least two thirds of the blanks are said to be reading the text well enough for independent study.

By clozing a passage of text selectively, the teacher is able to focus student attention on specific word slots for different instructional purposes.

Consider this example of clozing to teach author point of view:

1. Introduce the lesson by providing the following on a handout or presenting it to the class with an overhead. Tell them that this text is from a manual on bicycle safety. It was written by officials in a state department of transportation for use in the schools.

Drive close to the right side of _____ (1) _____, single file, and pass _____ (2) _____ cars with care. Sit _____ (3) _____ the bicycle seat when _____ (4) _____, and never carry extra _____ (5) _____—no "trick" riding. Never _____(6) _____ rides on other vehicles. _____ (7) carry loads which prevent _____ (8) _____ from keeping at least (9) _____ hand on the handlebars _____ (10) _____ all times.

2. Ask students to fill in each blank with the correct missing word, if you have used handouts; otherwise do it as a group activity with class discussion. Use the overhead. (We have numbered the blanks here for our discussion; you needn't do so when you cloze text for your students.)

Many students will select the word *road* for number one, when the actual missing word is *street*. You can discuss synonyms and whether they should count. After all, *road* fits the blank just as readily as does *street*, or does it? Read on. Most should get *parked* for number two, although some might choose *all*. A little mental imagery of a bicyclist passing a car going 55 mph helps with this one! *On* for number three and *riding* for number four should come fairly easily. Many, possibly most, of your students will want to assert that *riders* is the appropriate word for number five. Here you should remind them that this text was written by a state government official, not by a teacher or professional writer. Point out how in most driver's training manuals issued by the state, people drive *vehicles* rather than *cars*! Government booklets and pamphlets tend to be written in formal, stiff, even stodgy style. Bicyclists ride on *streets* rather than *roads*; they carry *passengers* rather than *riders*, even though the term *riders* is perfectly acceptable in most contexts.

It is true that the author has a responsibility to keep his reading audience in mind when writing. It is also true, however, that **the reader has a responsibility to always keep the author in mind**—who he or she is, for whom the text is probably most intended, what kind of language and writing style this particular author is likely to appropriate to the task, and so on.

3. Provide students with a handout of a text you have written for the students to cloze. For each blank provide them with a choice of words (multiple-choice cloze). They must choose an appropriate word for each blank from the choices given. Following is an example of this kind of text passage:

The _____ detective walked _____ down
(handsome, cowardly)   (sleazily, crisply)

the _____ street. He peered ahead _____
(comfortable, dark)   (bravely, hesitantly)

as he wondered what was in store for him. The job Lady Wimbly had

hired him for was _____ . His behavior then was totally
(dangerous, simple)

_____ .
(ludicrous, warranted)

After students have clozed the passage, have them exchange with class-mates and compare each other's rewrites.

Discuss how choice of words determined, shaped, or reflected our attitude toward the detective and his job. Also note that once a choice was made for the first blank space, that choice dictated our remaining choices (if we remained consistent in our description.)

Discuss the important role of adjectives and adverbs in shaping the author's and the reader's point of view about the text.

4. Provide students with additional passages to cloze *without* choices of words, so that they must come up with their own words. Remind them to choose vocabulary that helps shape the reader's point of view.

5. Have students create their own text passages, then delete key words and exchange with classmates for completion. Steps four and five should be followed by group or class discussion about how word choice shaped the reader's perception or point of view.

Although this particular model lesson was written for upper grade level students, you can easily see where appropriate adjustments can be made to suit lower or even higher grade level classes.

Using Semantic Mapping

Of the various techniques most widely advocated for improving reading vocabulary through formal instruction, semantic mapping is probably the most popular. Sometimes referred to as *semantic webbing* or *networking*, semantic mapping possesses a number of advantages for making it a very useful teaching approach.

It is actually quite simple in both principle and practice. In brief, the teacher identifies a key topic or labeling term and writes it on the board. Students are encouraged to think of words associated with this term. As words are volunteered, the teacher writes them on the board around the key center term. These words are circled and connected to the central term with a line.

After a number of words have been volunteered, the arrangement on the board begins to look like a spoked wagon wheel; then, as more words are added and lines indicating their relationships to each other are drawn, the structure begins to look like a web or flow chart (depending upon the graphics style and design capabilities of the teacher).

As a prereading technique, semantic mapping is an excellent way to introduce selection vocabulary and discuss word meanings and word relationships. Further, it is an excellent means for activating prior knowledge and building new background knowledge prior to text reading. These benefits are in addition to the cognitive operations of classification and abstraction that take place. Semantic mapping does a number of things that bear directly not only upon the acquisition of new reading vocabulary, but also upon the entire domain of reading comprehension.

Following is a series of steps for using semantic mapping as a technique during the prereading phase of instruction. Adjustments and modifications can be made to fit the technique to your own classroom needs.

1. Select a word central to the theme or main idea of the text. Write the word in a circle on the board. For example:

2. Ask students to think of words that would likely appear in a story or text about such a topic. Write those words in smaller circles surrounding

the word you have on the board. Connect the volunteered words to the center word with lines or spokes, for example:

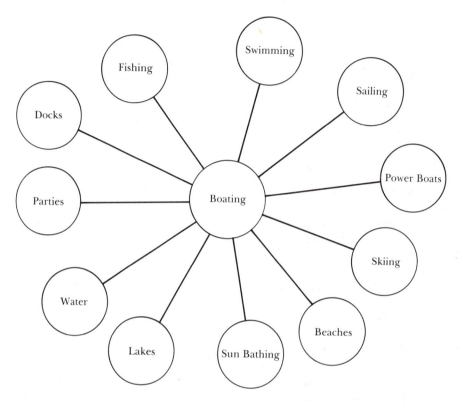

3. As words are volunteered, encourage students to talk about them, use them, and so on. During the discussion, you may end up deleting some words and adding others.

4. After you have generated a range of words, discuss how certain of them relate in particular ways to others. For example, *water, lakes,* and *beaches* are all elements needed for boating, and they are places or things. The other terms, e.g., *skiing, sun bathing,* and so on, are human activities. Show these connections between the two different groups of words by drawing dotted lines between those that go together. Your map will look something like the above illustration, but with dotted lines connecting like words.

As an alternative, list columns under your semantic map with labels heading each column. For the map, we would probably have only two columns, for example, places/things and human activities.

Remember! **Keep students on track**. One weakness of the semantic mapping technique is that class discussion can turn into a brainstorming session, with some students eager to take it in unprofitable directions. To keep students on track, use questions designed to get them to use the vocabulary that has been generated to glean important background information to help them in their reading.

Using Feature Analysis

Vocabulary feature analysis bears some similarities to semantic mapping in that it encourages learners to examine features or properties of concept words, to look at word relationships, and to categorize words according to features.

The roots of feature analysis are in the studies of the 1960s and 1970s, when researchers were interested in children's acquisition of the various features of concept words, the kind of features acquired, and the order of the acquisition. Humans, for example, have many different sets of features. We can talk about the physical features, i.e., legs, arms, head. We can talk about behavior features, i.e., eating, sleeping, and so on. We can talk about emotional features, i.e., loving, caring, hurting, angering. In addition, humans fit into different categories, i.e., man, woman, father, sister, teacher.

In feature analysis, we encourage learners to examine vocabulary in terms of selected, general features or attributes. For example, take the category of *pets*. We normally think of dog and cat as the most common. Now think of some of the features they have in common, e.g., four legs, hair, similar sounds, similar eating habits.

A chart with related words in the left-hand column and features across the top is graphically effective. For example:

Vehicles	4 Wheels	Fast	Riders	Cargo	For Work
Cars	+	+	+	+	+
Trucks	+	−	+	+	+
Motocycles	−	+	+	−	−
Tractors	−	−	−	−	+

If we use a + in each box where the word possesses that feature and a − in each box where it does not, then we get a pattern like that depicted here. Discussion will probably center on which features to appropriate to which terms. Some may point out, for example, how some trucks are fast and some trucks are not used for work. Identification of features and assignment of features to new words make for excellent discussion of new reading vocabulary.

The following steps outline one way you can use feature analysis as a reading vocabulary activity:

1. Write a short list (five or six words at most) in a column on the board. Choose words that are related, with concepts that have many things in common. Categories of things are easiest to begin with. For example, buildings, clothing, animals, white-collar jobs, and so on.
2. Ask students to choose any one of the words and think of a feature it has. Write that feature as a heading to the right of your column. As students generate more attributes for the word, write them down as separate headings. After you have a few features listed, draw vertical and horizontal lines to divide your list and headings into columns and rows. You should end up with a large box similar to that depicted earlier.
3. Go through each of the words with the class, moving to the right in each row placing a + or − in each box as the class decides whether the feature is applicable or not.
4. After the box is completed, discuss the vocabulary in general, pointing out that although the words might have one feature in common, none of them share all the features.

Additional activities using this technique can include handouts of prepared *empty* feature analysis charts for students to use individually or in pairs to generate their own lists and features. The larger the number of words and features, the more challenging the activity.

As with semantic mapping, students must use fundamental cognitive operations of classification and abstraction to complete this activity. Also, both semantic mapping and feature analysis fit well with the predict-test-conclude questioning strategy; they also fit quite well in the topic-centered reading vocabulary development strategy.

Using Analogies

The techniques and activities for using analogies as discussed in the chapter on questioning strategies also hold for this section. Therefore, I shall not devote as much attention to them here. However, note that analogizing and working formal analogical statements reflect many of the same advantages found in semantic mapping and feature analysis. Analogies require perhaps a greater range of cognitive operations, especially for the more complex analogical forms and uses.

Johnson and Baumann (1984) identify ten types of analogical relationships that can be expressed in formal analogical statements. They are:

1. Characteristics: Rain is to wet as sun is to dry.
2. Part/Whole: Leaf is to tree as feather is to bird.

3. Whole/Part: Cup is to handle as clock is to hands.
4. Location: Teacher is to classroom as sailor is to ship.
5. Action/Agent: Run is to track as swim is to pool.
6. Agent/Action: Teacher is to student as doctor is to patient.
7. Class or Synonym: Smell is to sniff as see is to look.
8. Familial: Uncle is to nephew as aunt is to niece.
9. Grammatical: Hear is to heard as see is to seen.
10. Temporal: Fifth is to first as twenty-fifth is to fifth.

In designing analogical activities for students, this range of conceptual relationships should be kept in mind to assure that students are implicitly pressured to ply the cognitive range in their work.

The cloze can be used selectively to make the analogies easier or more difficult. That is, you may require learners to think of only one word to complete a relationship or you may require them to think of two words, both on one side of the analogy or one on each side. Consider these examples:

_____ is to hot as black is to cold.

Red is to hot as _____ is to _____.

Or,

Red is to _____ as black is to _____.

and,

_____ is to hot as black is to _____.

It is important to keep in mind that analogies such as these should not be done in isolation from the text for the most part. That is, important relationships and vocabulary in the text should be used to build the analogy problems.

In addition, analogies should be done only on an irregular basis for short periods of instructional time. It does not take very long for this activity—which can be a great deal of fun initially—to become boring! But it has considerable potential if used judiciously.

III Models

This category of reading vocabulary instruction is designed primarily for long-range acquisition of reading vocabulary and for assisting in low-level dictionary entries or shifting entries in lower-level dictionaries. Also, it represents possibly the best opportunity for the teacher to work with students to develop positive attitudes about words and what they can do for us. This category includes language games and language play, along with activities and techniques more closely allied with our second category, DII.

The difference between DII activities and techniques and those in III has to do primarily with the timing and spacing of approaches.

Most of the ideas in III possess greater flexibility and irregularity as a whole, which will become more obvious as we get into them.

Using Etymology

Word history, or etymology, is one of the more intriguing areas of language study. We have a chance to learn not only more about our language but also more about ourselves and how we use language. Giving students an opportunity to look at how words are built and change over time not only aids in their vocabulary growth, but also provides insight into what it means to be human.

Techniques and activities built around etymology also represent an excellent opportunity for study of the dictionary, its development, and its uses. Students can learn that there is more information in dictionaries than just word definitions. Of course, if students have access to and knowledge of dictionaries such as the *Oxford English Dictionary* (which contains over 400,000 definitions, plus a great deal of historical and other related information), they can do more with etymology than younger children, who do not have the maturity or dictionary training to handle them. Therefore, many of these activities are aimed at the upper elementary and secondary grades. However, some techniques and activities included here are applicable in lower grades with little adjustment.

Using Semantic Change

Words change over time in various ways. Following are the most conspicuous types of changes:

1. *Generalization:* A word moves from specialized use to broader or more general use. For example, a *manuscript* was originally a "hand-written copy" of something. Now the term is used to refer to any nonprinted copy.
2. *Specialization:* A word moves in meaning from more general to more specific. At one time the word *starve* simply meant "to die," but now it means "to die of hunger."
3. *Pejoration:* A word takes on more negative connotations with the passage of time. Many years ago the word *lust* was used to describe any pleasure. Now its use is more restricted to physical passion.
4. *Amelioration:* A word takes on more positive connotations with the passage of time. *Steward* comes from two German words meaning "keeper of the stie"— one who tended pigs. Now it serves a more dignified role.
5. *Concretization:* A word takes on more concrete meaning and gives up its original abstract role. *Honor* has moved from meaning simply "to pay esteem to someone or something" to being used as a title for a judge.
6. *Abstraction:* A word sacrifices some of its original concrete uses and takes on more abstract connotations. A *lemon* is more than just a fruit!

7. *Radiation:* A word generates a variety of independent meanings by analogy. For example, *head* has moved from being just the top part of a body to also being the leader of a company or the top part of a beer.
8. *Euphemism:* A word is phased out of use because of negative connotations. People don't *die*, but instead *pass away*.
9. *Hyperbole:* A word's primary meaning is weakened or even lost because of overuse. "Wow! He's really *radical*.
10. *Transference:* The meaning of a word shifts from the roles of subject to object or from object to subject. *Curious* can now be used to describe a person or an object, e.g., a *curious* person or a *curious* business.

Ask your students to find examples of each type of semantic change. This can be a combined dictionary and personal experience assignment. Examples of euphemisms, hyperbole, radiation, and transference abound. The other categories might be more difficult to exemplify without the aid of a good dictionary.

Remind students that there are a number of excellent sources for this assignment. Television, radio, ads in magazines and newspapers, current slang on the playground or at social events are all excellent. For children in the lower grades use only two or three categories. Many first and second graders have mastered a considerable body of slang that capitalizes heavily upon euphemism and hyperbole. Discuss the words students bring to class. Emphasize the fact that language is constantly changing and we are all contributing!

Using Word Formation

Another etymologically oriented activity provides learners with the following categories of word formation techniques:

1. *Word role shift:* Nouns become verbs, e.g., *nail*; verbs become nouns, e.g., *dump*; inanimate verbs take animate roles, e.g., "Bud drinks good."
2. *Compounding: Book* and *store* to *bookstore.*
3. *Clipping or deleting: Gymnasium* to *gym; telephone* to *phone.*
4. *Back formation:* -ate verbs to -ation nouns, e.g., *deviate* to *deviation.*
5. *Blending: Hotel* and *motor* to *motel;* acronyms, e.g., *Sunoco.*
6. *Coining: normalcy, gerrymander.*

We form new words in our language by using one or more of these word formation techniques. Sometimes words get changed quite rapidly, sometimes only over many years.

Some activities involving word formation follow:

● Keep your notebook with you for a week. Record examples of words that you hear or see that have been changed using one of these techniques.

- Think of new words that we need but do not have (*coining*). Have a contest to see who can come up with the best name for:

  a. That thin line of dust always left from the dustpan when you dust, no matter how hard you try.

  b. A group of something that we do not have a group name for. For example, we have a *school of fish, herd of elephants,* and *gaggle of geese.* What might we call a bunch of slugs (a slime of slugs?) or a bunch of priests (a mass of priests?)?
- Use a dictionary to find more examples of each category.

Using Dialect

One of the more important things students can learn about language is that there is no *correct* and *incorrect* language but rather *appropriate* and *inappropriate* language. They also need to know that different people in different parts of our country use language differently. Equally well-educated people will disagree on the acceptable way to use language in any given context. The sooner children learn about these differences in language use, the sooner they will use language appropriate to the context and purpose of the occasion.

An excellent acitivity to incorporate into the year's reading vocabulary instruction follows:

1. Poll your class to find out how many have relatives or friends who live in other parts of the country. Usually there are a few with someone of like age who lives in a different dialect region.
2. Have one of your students tape a reading of text (a couple of pages will do). Make an extra copy of the tape and make a copy of the text.
3. Mail the tape, a copy of the text, and a cover letter to the teacher of the faraway student. Explain that you are studying language use around the country. Ask the teacher if he or she would have a student tape a reading of the same text and return the tape to you.
4. Play the returned tape in class. Talk about language differences between your class's language use and that on the tape returned from afar.

Multiple tapes can be sent out if you wish to build this into a bigger project.

FINAL COMMENTS

I would like to highlight a few important points on the development of reading vocabulary.

1. Acquisition and development of reading vocabulary is a long-range operation. Initially we build this vocabulary from oral language, and, we continue to use oral language to facilitate our acquisition and development of additional reading vocabulary throughout the years.

2. Effective growth in reading vocabulary occurs when learners are involved in two important learning contexts; direct instruction incorporating solid teaching strategies, techniques, and activities designed to meet the various demands of reading; a literacy-rich setting with ample materials; and an ongoing, positive attitude about literacy and its place in our lives. As the years progress and the learner internalizes the formalized processes of vocabulary acquisition, engages in wide-ranging speaking, writing, and reading activities, and comes to value the power and potential of written language, the growth of reading vocabulary becomes a natural part of literacy expansion.

In short, good readers know how to teach themselves new reading vocabulary. They know in which of their dictionaries to make entries, and how.

3. We must recognize the various internal dictionaries that students possess, the different roles these dictionaries play, and the different nature of the entry and exit levels within each. We must teach to the students' needs for particular reading vocabulary and not just for reading vocabulary in general.

4. The growth of students' reading vocabulary requires a total commitment to the reading program, if the best possible development of reading vocabulary for all students is to occur. The responsibility of the individual teachers becomes an important part of a larger commitment: the home, community, school, and classroom must be involved.

The ultimate result from conscientious effort could be the best reading programs possible.

ADDITIONAL SELECTED READINGS

BUSH, C. (1978). *Language remediation and expansion.* Tucson: Communication Skill Buildings, Inc.

DICKSON, P. (1982). *Words.* New York: Delacorte Press.

DURKIN, D. (1976). *Teaching word identification.* Boston: Allyn and Bacon.

ESPY, W. R. (1975). *Words at play.* New York: Clarkson Potter.

FARB, P. (1975). *Word play.* New York: Alfred A. Knopf.

GRAVES, M. ET AL. (1985). Educational perspectives. *Journal of the College of Education/University of Hawaii at Manoa, 23, no. 1* (entire issue devoted to vocabulary).

JOHNSON, D. AND PEARSON, P. D. (1984). *Teaching reading vocabulary.* New York: Holt, Rinehart and Winston.

PARTRIDGE, E. (1961). *A dictionary of slang and unconventional English: Two volumes in one.* New York: Macmillan.

SPERLING, S. K. (1977). *Poplollies and bellibones.* New York: Potter.

WOOD, K. D. AND ROBINSON, N. (1983). Vocabulary, language and prediction: A prereading strategy. *The Reading Teacher,* 392-395.

REFERENCES

ANDERSON, R. and FREEBODY, P. (1977). *Vocabulary knowledge and reading* (Technical Report no. 11). Urbana, Ill.: Center for the Study of Reading, University of Illinois.

BECK, I. L., and McKEOWN, M. (1985). Teaching vocabulary: Making the instruction fill the goal. *Educational Perspectives, 23,* 11-15.

GIRVETZ, H. (1963). *The evolution of liberalism.* New York: Collier Books.

JOHNSON, D. (1984). Expanding vocabulary through classification. In J. Baumann and D. Johnson, *Reading instruction and the beginning teacher.* Minneapolis: Burgess.

NAGY, W. and HERMAN, P. (1985). Incidental vs. instructional approaches to increasing reading vocabulary. *Educational Perspectives, 23,* 16-21.

SMITH, M. K. (1941). Measurement of the size of general English vocabulary through the elementary grades and high school. *General Psychological Monographs, 24,* 311-345.

VYGOTSKY, L. (1962). *Thought and language.* Cambridge, Mass.: MIT Press.

Self-Monitoring

READING AND THE *META* WORLD

I recently read an interesting and challenging book— *The Name of the Rose* by Umberto Eco. Set in the 14th century, the book is about a series of bizarre murders of monks in a monastary in Italy. The book requires readers to plunge into the religious history of the period, i.e., the split in the papacy, the emergence of a multitude of orders with their own commitments and ideologies, the contentious political history of the time. In fact, it is a superb example of the importance of background knowledge to text comprehension; in this book, the plot is tightly tied to the actual history of the period. For readers to immerse themselves seriously in this book, they must try to master at least key aspects of the period's history. A second reading of the book confirms the idea that the more you know prior to the reading, the more you take away from the reading.

No more than a third of the way into the book, I realized that after reading a particularly complex and information-loaded paragraph, I did not know what I had just read! I knew the meanings of the individual words and I knew where I was in the unfolding plot, but I had no idea of what I had just read. Why not? Too much information? Cognitive overload? Convoluted syntax on the part of the author? Simply not concentrating? Why did I not understand what I had just read?

Clearly, there was no point in continuing in this state of ignorance, so I stopped—as any sensible reader would—and reread the paragraph. This decision to reread was made unconsciously. I was monitoring myself as I read to make sure that I adequately understood the content, otherwise there would be no point in reading further.

During the past decade or so, reading educators have devoted more time to the study of this area of the reading process, i.e., the reader's *self-monitoring* during the reading act; what it is and how it is done. Although this is a new area of study and there is much yet to learn, reading authorities agree that since it is clear that good readers engage in self-monitoring, it is, at least, an important facility they have in common. Apparently it is a critical ability necessary for effective reading comprehension.

To engage in self-monitoring, the reader must employ metacognitive skills. That is, the reader must be able to think about his or her own thinking during the reading act. *Meta* prefixes many words familiar to teachers of reading, e.g., language, linguistics, and comprehension. Literally, *metacognition* means "to think about your own thinking"; *meta-comprehension* means "to think about your own comprehension." (These terms, *metacognition* and *metacomprehension*, are often used loosely as synonyms by reading educators.) *Metalanguage*, logically enough, means "to use language to describe or talk about language." When we teach formal grammar to our students, i.e., ask them to identify parts of speech, diagram sentences, and so on, we require them to use metalanguage, and we expect them to employ metalinguistic skills.

The *meta* area is rich for both research and instruction; it is one of the most conspicuous manifestations of the merger of thought and language. Ability to exploit the two in unison is basically what reading is all about.

Research in literacy development has indicated strong correlations between early metalinguistic awareness and later ability to read (Mason, 1984; and others). That is, preschoolers who know the character, purpose, and contours of print, the functions of a book, and the general features of plot and story development are more likely to be effective readers once they enter school than will be their counterparts who lack these metalinguistic skills. This research reinforces once more the importance of maintaining a rich literacy environment in the homes of young children, of providing them with books and magazines, of reading to them regularly, and of engaging them in talk about what has been read or is being read.

Let's examine some of the key ideas in the *meta* world that the reader must master to become self-monitoring.

Linguisitic awareness   In some senses, a child is linguistically aware as soon as he or she knows that language has a function other than that of noise-making generally. Most linguists, however, concur that the most conspicuous, observable evidence of linguistic awareness is when a child automatically self-corrects a mistake in oral language. For example, a child might begin an utterance with "want I a . . ." and then stop and correct to "I want a drink." This self-monitoring of the structure and meaning of one's own utterances occurs quite early in most children—well before three years—and develops naturally as long as the child is in a language environment. It need not be taught directly.

Metalinguistic awareness Being metalinguistically aware means different things to different people. A child who knows that writing in the English language is linear and goes from left to right and from the top of a page to the bottom of the page, that a book has covers and a front and a back, a right side up and an upside-down position, and that there is correspondence between oral utterances and words in print can be said to be metalinguistically aware. Interestingly enough, there are some children entering school who do not possess the above knowledge. And there are many children—especially through the primary grades—who possess only slightly more sophisticated levels of metalinguistic awareness. For example, even into the primary grades some children have difficulty identifying *word* as a concept in print (Gough, 1984); and others).

This should not be surprising when one considers the difference in the nature and functions of language for children prior to school entry and the nature and functions of language in the classroom. Some reading authorities, e.g., John Downing, refer to the latter language as the *instructional register*. Children use language normally for *object reference* purposes only. "I want a banana." "I don't want to go to bed yet." "Can I go to Jimmie's house to play? These utterances constantly refer to elements, events, and activities in the real, objective world—elements, events, and activities that bear directly on the child's immediate physical wants and needs.

Once children enter the classroom, however, the focus of the language and even its fundamental structure and character shift. Terms such as *word, letter, sentence* are used. The instructional register is primarily a metalinguistic system. In beginning reading instruction, the teacher uses a lot of language that has other language rather than the objective world as reference. It is removed and highly abstract language. Little wonder then that beginning reading instruction can often be so tricky and confusing for the child.

Several years ago, a language development expert told of working with a group of second-grade children with reading difficulties in a West Coast city school system. As the children practiced reading silently in small groups at the beginning of the school year, the teacher moved among them. A small child motioned her over and asked, "What is this word?" (pointing to the word *what* in the book). "*What,*" said the teacher. "This word," stated the child, smiling and once more pointing to the word *what* in the book. The teacher's assessment was that any second-grade child with that degree of metalinguistic sensitivity should not have reading difficulties; and indeed, within a short time and with proper instruction, the child was reading quite effectively.

What authorities do not agree upon, however, is how best to develop metalinguistic sensitivity or awareness, especially in the primary grades. Some advocate direct instruction in the metalanguage. For example, some recommend direct instruction in the instructional register at the beginning of school. Children are taught early on the meaning of terms such as *word, letter, sentence, line,* and so on.

Others argue that metalinguistic sensitivity for the child evolves from and through language use for functional purposes. In particular, language play—riddles, puns, palendromes, and so on—in a variety of language use contexts is the most effective means for developing this ability.

A reasonable posture incorporates both views—provide direct instruction when appropriate *and* provide a rich language use environment which encourages oral and written expression for a wide variety of purposes and contexts.

Metacognitive awareness "Knowing that you know" comes relatively late in child development. Piaget noted that preoperational-stage children know how to think. However, it is not until they enter the stage of concrete operations that they can think about their own thinking. For reading comprehension, there is perhaps no single more important ability than that which enables one to analyze, critique, ponder, and generally explore one's own thinking during the reading act.

The task of the reader is always twofold: To constantly examine and question the author and the author's intent and, at the same time, to analyze one's own thinking during the reading.

Good readers do this. Poor readers do not and often do not know that they should.

One view of metacomprehension holds it to be the unique application of metacognition to the reading act. Unlike metalinguistic sensitivity, however, metacomprehension skills are both subtler and more complex. They are easier to think of in global terms but easier also to leave out of reading instruction; few basal reading programs attend to them in any particular or direct fashion. Although there is wide reference to metacognition and metacomprehension in the professioal literature, few commercially developed materials or programs, even exclusive of basals, provide many ideas for teachers of reading.

Part of the difficulty is tied to the complexity of the concept itself in knowing what to do with what we already know about metacognition and reading instruction that incorporates or builds upon metacognition.

However, there are some specific guidelines to help us make decisions about the uses of metacognitive/comprehension ideas to improve reading comprehension instruction.

1. Metacognition should be emphasized as an important aspect of reading instruction throughout grades K–12. Although we have focused upon its role in early reading development, remember that levels of sophistication in the employment of metacognitive skills during reading can be increased and refined throughout the grades. In fact, in many respects, one of the most fruitful periods for direct instruction in all of the *meta* areas is during the middle and secondary grades.

2. Instructional techniques and strategies incorporating metacognition should be taught directly as well as informally throughout grades K–12.

3. Some of the more productive areas for incorporating metacognitive techniques and strategies into instruction are in the teaching of study skills and in the content areas generally. In fact (and in some senses at least), we can think of study skills as synonymous with metacomprehension; for reading, from the critical and analytical perspective, is what study skills are. On the other hand, the content areas represent the richest kind of familiar text—narrative and especially expository writing.

4. Role-playing and peer-modeling are some of the more productive techniques to incorporate metacognition into reading comprehension instruction. By allowing the students to play teacher, you place them in a context where they must think about why and how they are going to teach something, i.e., they must think about how they will expect others to think. The only way that can be done is to think about how we ourselves think.

5. The use of writing in reading instruction, when done wisely and appropriately, nearly always involves students in metacognition—for the act of writing itself, regardless of context, requires the writer to think about what is to be written. More mature and sophisticated writers also think about what is being written "as the pen alights" and immediately after the alighting by echoes of what has just been thought through.

6. Teaching reading with a *strong metacognitive mind set* enables the teacher to more easily capitalize upon those spur-of-the-moment opportunities that occur daily and which can sometimes make the difference betweeen a learner understanding or not understanding text, not to mention capitalizing upon or missing an opportunity to develop a critical skill for effective reading.

Self-Probing Questions

What do effective readers do while reading? The answer is simple. They think. They think about what they know about the subject in the text being read. They think about this knowledge in relation to what they are reading. They think about what is happening in the reading. They also predict what is likely to occur in the coming text. If the content is of substantial interest or importance, they also try to fit the new information into their lives.

Although there are clearly certain idiosyncracies in individual readers and how they approach a text, there are also certain generalizable characteristics which are found in all effective readers.

Good readers question constantly both before and throughout the reading. They begin, in fact, by asking what we shall call *self-probing questions*. Why am I reading this selection? How difficult will it be? What do I expect to remember from the reading? What do I want to retain? What is optional information? What clues to content and complexity of the material can be found in the title or subtitles? Shall I bother to take notes, highlight text, or write in the margins of the book? Notice that some of these questions are asked during the prereading period. Others are asked during the actual reading.

Consider the following newspaper article, for example:

PASSENGERS RESCUED

KLAWOCK, Alaska—A luxury cruise ship struck a reef in Alaska yesterday and tore a foot-long gash in its hull, but the Indian fishermen safely evacuated the 143 passengers from the listing vessel. The 295-foot, Bahamian-registered North Star "cut on the wrong side on a buoy and got stuck on a big long reef " about 10 miles west of Klawock, said Frank Peratrovich, fire and rescue dispatcher in the Indian village.

The cruise ship, which carried 143 passengers and 60 crew members, began taking on water through the gash faster than the vessel's machinery could pump it out, Coast Guard Petty Officer Glen Rosenholm said.

The Coast Guard Cutter Cape Hatteras and a Coast Guard helicopter, rushed to save the North Star. But Klawock residents and fishermen beat the Coast Guard to the accident, helping passengers a few dozen at a time onto small boats, Peratrovich said.

The Honolulu Advertiser,
Sat., August 9, 1986

Now consider our prior-to-reading self-probing questions:

1. Why am I reading this selection? Most likely we would read a newspaper article for general information and out of curiosity. In this case, however, assume that you had a friend or relative on a cruise ship in Alaska. Notice how the remainder of your questions and your general approach to the reading change.
2. How difficult will it be? Not very, since it is a newspaper article and not an editorial. We know that the readability level will be relatively low.
3. What do I expect to get from the reading? What should I retain? What is optional? Assuming we are reading for general information, we are probably curious about the conditions leading to the accident, injuries, nature of the rescue, and other unique factors.
4. What clues are in the title or subtitles? The headline suggests an accident involving a means of transportation. The Alaska by-line helps narrow it further in probability of type.
5. Should I take notes? Probably not, unless I have a special reason for remembering the information in detail.

Although the self-probing questions may vary somewhat, the effective reader engages in extensive metacognitive operations before beginning to read.

Techniques and Activities

● Prior to assigning a story, article, report, or work in a content area textbook, have students respond to each of the self-probing questions described earlier using only the following information. Although this activity can be either oral (with class discussion) or written (with the students writing their responses first), a mixture of the two provides greater variety and flexibility.

1. A story is assigned in class. Its title is "Lost in the Forest." A test will be given after reading the story.
2. A chapter in the social studies text entitled "The Balance of Power: The Main Branches of the Federal Government" is assigned. Class discussion will follow.
3. A student opts to read a novel entitled *The Ghost Ship of the North Sea*, a mystery about an abandoned ship found at sea with gold bullion aboard. The reading is selected and not assigned. No reports or test is expected.
4. A contract is to be signed by you; it covers an agreement to repay a loan you are obtaining to make a purchase. The contract contains terms of the agreement to repay and default and penalty clauses.
5. You are preparing an important meal with an entree you have not made before. Your guests are arriving for dinner in a short time, so you do not have long to choose recipes. You already have the ingredients necessary for a few you are considering. You are going to read the recipe entitled "Poached Salmon with Lemon Butter."

Notice how the nature of our self-probing questions and the seriousness with which we approach the reading changes according to our felt needs. Numbers four and five are much more likely to generate extended self-probing questions than are the first three. Discuss the reasons for this with your students.

Predictions

Good readers hypothesize about what will likely appear in a text, and they make predictions about events or outcomes to appear in the text on an ongoing basis. These predictions are derived from prior knowledge, deducing likely outcomes from information given or often implicit in the text, and from applying commonsense inductive principles of cause and effect in their reading.

It is not so important that these predictions or hypotheses be accurate as it is that they simply be made. Good readers use predictions as benchmarks against which to measure or test information in the text. No predictions, no effective comprehension—it is as simple as that.

Techniques and Activities

● Provide students with a variety of titles for stories to be read. Ask them to predict what the story is about. The prediction should be made in the form of a statement that completes the sentence whose beginning is provided. Ask them also to make one or two predictions about events or things that might happen in a story with such a title. Finally, for each prediction made, ask them to provide supporting statements indicating why they projected what they did.

This can be an oral or written activity. You can write titles on the chalkboard or with an overhead projector and then engage students in discussions that require them to justify their predictions. Or, you can prepare an activity sheet in a format suitable for duplicating. For example, the following models can be used with modification to make each appropriate for different grade levels.

Title: "Fishing at the Farm Pond"
Prediction: I believe this story will be about _____

_____

_____

Jusification: I believe the story will be about this because

_____

_____

_____

Prediction: One thing that I think will happen in this story is

_____

_____

Justification: I believe this will happen because _____

_____

_____

● Provide students with titles of articles from newspapers (actual or fabricated) and ask them to make predictions about the content and provide supporting statements of justification for their predictions. Since this is nonfiction, expository text additional observations regarding the significance or importance of such information is also called for. For example, the earlier format can simply be elaborated somewhat.

Newspaper Article Title: "Two Mountain Climbers Lost in Avalanche on Mt. Baker"

Prediction: I think this article will be about _____

_____

_____

Justification: I think the article will be about this because

_____

_____

Supporting-Detail Predictions: Here are some of the important things

I think that will be talked about in this article:

1. _____

2. _____

3. _____

Importance Justification: I think the information in this article is

important because _____

_____

_____

● Provide students with your own predictions about information in a newspaper article based only upon the title. Have them agree or disagree with your predictions and justify their reasoning. For example:

Newspaper Article Title: "Two Mountain Climbers Lost in Avalanche on Mt. Baker"

Prediction: I think this will be an article about two climbers who became careless and lost their way on a mountain climb. They stumbled into an avalanche path and were covered up.

Agree or Disagree and Why: _____

_____

_____

_____

Or, I think this will be an article about a tragic unavoidable accident of two experienced mountain climbers.

Agree or Disagree and Why: _____

_____

_____

_____

_____

This particular activity is excellent for developing prereading discussions designed to activate prior knowledge or to develop background knowledge, as well as to provide learners with necessary skills in developing hypothesizing approaches to their reading.

Notice that the student is asked to hypothesize or predict using information that is primarily *implicit*—information that the student infers from what he or she knows about a given subject or what he or she knows about the world. Only this implicit information keyed to clues in the titles and one's past experience (with events or ideas tied to the title) help the reader make predictions.

The more *explicit* the information given to the reader, the closer the reader's predictions get to formal inferences or conclusions. In fact, in some senses, all predictions are inferences of a sort. We predict based upon what we know implicitly or from the few clues we get in a title or other type of text adjunct, e.g., picture, graph, footnote, and so on. To form our predictions, we have reasoned inductively from an array of data of varying degrees of saliency to our topic.

For example, assume that I observe that the last fifty cars I have seen were all foreign built. I can *predict,* based upon the data and what I have accumulated over the years, that the next car I see will be foreign built. I have made a prediction or have formulated a hypothesis. However, I have also drawn an inductive inference. *All* predictions are inferences. They are inferences drawn from implicit or explicit information and more commonly from a combination of both.

Generally speaking, prereading and reading of the text in the earliest stages require the reader to make predictions on the basis of implicit information, while later predictions, after the reader has acquired more data from the text, can be based upon a higher proportion of explicit information. Both kinds of predictions are necessary. It is helpful for the reader to know the difference between implicit and explicit data and to think about that difference while reading the text.

One way to help students distinguish between the two kinds of data is to vary the prediction activities you provide to incorporate both kinds. For example, notice the following list of possible titles:

"The Day I Spent in New York City without Any Clothes!"

Our background information about the social practice of wearing clothes, what we know about New York City, and the exclamation mark at the end of the title all help us to predict that this will probably be a humorous piece about someone who either lost his or her clothing or had it stolen, and how the person had to cope in a variety of funny contexts without the clothing for one day.

"Don't Go Ice Skating in Warm Late-Spring Weather"

This is likely to be a text about someone who either fell through the ice while skating or nearly did.

"Ice Skating during Warm Spring Days"

In this title, the fewer explicit details reduce considerably our ability to make predictions as powerfully as we did in the previous title.

Remember, in all of the instructional activities and techniques offered here, the purpose is to encourage students to think and to think about their thinking! Their ability to draw a correct inference or make a correct prediction before or during their reading is instructionally less important than their development of an ongoing, critical analysis of the author's reasoning and of their own thinking during the reading act.

Reconstructive Memory

During the 1970s a number of reading educators pursued research in what is often called *reconstructive memory*. Subjects were asked to listen to the reading of a text— usually a short one, two, or three paragraphs in length. Sometimes these texts were contrived stories designed to reflect the most important attributes of story structures found in normal fiction. Other times they were nonfiction (excerpts from a newspaper or from a content areas textbook). Subjects were then asked to *reconstruct* the text by writing it as exactly as they could recall it without further benefit of seeing the text.

The reconstructed texts were collected; subjects were asked to recall the same text one or two times more over the next several days or weeks, without hearing the text again. These separate reconstructions were then compared, primarily to discover the changes that took place, the roles of short-term and long-term memory, the salience of particular mnemonic devices, and so on.

In addition to the data from this research, the instructional potential of reconstructive memory as a metacognitive technique has received attention. This is particularly intriguing because reconstructure memory can be used throughout most of the elementary and secondary grades; in addition, it possesses a range of instructional applications, all of which contribute to the exploitation of metacognitive skills in the reader. Some of these potential applications follow.

Techniques and Activities

● Follow these steps with appropriate modification to adjust for learner ability or grade level:

1. Choose a short newspaper article of three to four paragraphs (6th grade and up). Or, contrive a very short story or select one from a reader (primary grades/intermediate grades); be sure the story is well within the students' range of experience and interest.
2. Do not tell your students what the overall plan is for the activity. Tell them that you are going to read the entire text to them. You will do so slowly and clearly. They should listen carefully, pen and paper ready to use immediately after the reading is finished. Tell them that you will ask them to write the selection as accurately as possible, word for word, but you will not reread any of it or answer any questions about it after the reading. Be sure they know this is not a test!
3. Read the text aloud and ask them to write.
4. Collect their written reconstructions with names and dates on their papers. Keep the papers.
5. Two days later (one day in the primary grades), ask your students to recall the text the best that they can. Ask them to rewrite it once more. Be sure names and dates are on the papers.
6. Three days later ask your students to do one more rewrite. (The number of days between reconstruction can be varied somewhat to accommodate the school schedule or your teaching plans.) The actual time needed for each rewrite will probably not exceed ten or twelve minutes.
7. Assemble all of the student rewrites. Return each student's three papers.
8. Prepare a one-page handout for your students with the following information and give it to them along with a copy of the original text that you read to them.

HAND-OUT FOR STUDENTS

a. Place each of your papers side by side and read each, beginning with the first one you wrote. Think about how they are *alike* and how they are *different*.
b. On a sheet, list things, ideas, or events that are included in your first paper that are not in your other papers.
c. Count the number of particular statements and the number of generalizations in each of your papers. List the number of each type you have for each of your papers. How are your papers different? (Note that this step is only for students in the middle or secondary grades who know the difference between particular and general assertions or particular statements and generalizations.)
d. Compare each of your papers with the actual text your teacher read. Note the similarities and the differences between it and your papers.
e. Write a paper that tells what the most important things were that you remembered. Also tell what important information you forgot.

9. Pair students and have them compare their rewrites with each other. Ask them to note how their rewrites are alike and how they are different, i.e., what information both tended to remember, what information both forgot, how some things were important for one but not for the other, and so on.

10. Discuss the activity with the class. You should have excellent results, with your students anxious to share what they remembered and what they forgot.

Studies in reconstructive memory indicate that certain things predictably occur in reconstructions such as those described here. They can be summarized as follows:

- We tend to remember more details in the early reconstructions than in the late ones.
- There are more generalizations in the later reconstructions than in the early ones, since we tend to *fold in* detail for long-term memory storage.
- Some of the new generalizations created are built by collapsing or folding in original detail, and some generalizations derive from inferred or predicted information which was not provided directly in the reading.
- Some details are added which were *not* in the original at all nor specifically implied. We tend to add new information over time. Usually this new information is logical, i.e., it probably could fit into the text without destroying its integrity, but it is fictional. In other words, we tend to remember more than we were told to begin with!

Use these reconstruction findings as benchmarks in discussing your students' work with them.

Summarizing

The ability to summarize effectively—decribe the main ideas or content of a text in briefer form and, usually, in different language—has always been a favorite means to assess students' knowledge of text and to monitor students' progress through text. In addition, it is one of the most widely employed classroom teaching techniques. In fact, teachers often use summarizing to instruct even though its assessment or monitoring roles are likely to be dominant.

Over the years research has tended to support the instructional use of summarizing for improving reading comprehension (Day, 1980; and others). It can be an advance organizer during the prereading phase; during the postreading phase it can be a means of bringing closure to a reading lesson; and the learner can use it in a limited number of ways during the actual reading.

Although summarizing as an activity or teaching technique appears straightforward, it is not that simple. For one thing, it is difficult even to define the concept without using the term itself in the definition. Paraphrasing—restating an idea in different language—is usually involved in summarizing (although we usually ascribe more to summarizing than just restatement of an idea, as important as that ability might be). Also, we are often asked to paraphrase a statement or two, but we typically think of summarizing as an activity that addresses text longer than a few sentences.

In addition, it seems somewhat easier to summarize certain kinds or forms of text than others. Expository text tends to have a tighter logical structure than does narrative or poetic. For example, an expository paragraph is likely to contain an opening thesis assertion or main-idea sentence (also called *topic sentence*), followed by supporting detail in some order and a concluding sentence at the end of the paragraph. In fact, many students get in the habit of simply feeding back the first sentence of the paragraph to the teacher when asked to summarize the paragraph. However, the task is complicated when the paragraph has no topic sentence but rather an *oblique* thesis assertion which is implied in the paragraph, or when the paragraph is narrative rather than expository and not likely to have a topic sentence. However, even the idea of summarizing certain text forms sounds strange, (such as poetry) since one doesn't normally think of it as amenable to summarization.

These constraints notwithstanding, the teacher can do a number of things to incorporate summarizing into his or her teaching. However, the teacher should probably introduce the concept by demonstrating what it means rather than attempting to use a dictionary definition. Even this sort of definition by example may be difficult for children in the primary grades, since paraphrasing is an element of summarizing, and the ability to paraphrase by children before the ages of nine or ten is limited (Klein, 1973).

Some authorities, such as Brown and Day (1983), suggest that the reader goes through a specific set of processes in the summarizing act. One is *deletion*. In order to summarize effectively, the reader must delete unimportant or less important information. A second process is *superordination*. The reader uses general terms and statements, with details and facts from the original text folded in. (Recall our reconstructive memory activities!) A third process is *selection*. Important information statements are retained or revised only minimally. Fourth and finally, the effective summarizer employs *invention*. The reader invents or constructs new statements to effectively indicate ideas that are not necessarily stated directly in the text. Activities designed to help students develop and refine their skills in using these processes should be an ongoing part of a reading comprehension instruction plan.

A few general guidelines should be remembered when designing summarizing activities:

1. Try to keep summarizing activities for text that is a paragraph long or longer.
2. Introduce summarizing activities by using expository text, since it lends itself more readily to summarizing.
3. Remember to require students to summarize both orally, during classroom discussion, and in writing.

4. Use summarizing activities that incorporate writing at least twice a week throughout the school year.

Techniques and Activities

● Choose a sample of narrative or expository text in grade-level-appropriate materials, e.g., social studies and science textbooks, newspapers, basal readers. Type the text and duplicate it for student handout. Ask your students to draw lines through information which could be deleted if they were to summarize the text.

● Using the text from the above activity or a new text, have students underline the words and sentences most important to summarizing the text.

● Again, using the above text or a new one, ask students to write two or three general statements which use information and details from the text. These generalizations should give the reader a reasonably accurate picture of the main ideas in the text without benefit of specific detail.

● Assign students a selection of nonfiction text. Choose text where exposition is the dominant form and which is thus more amenable to summarization. Ask students to write a one-sentence summary for each paragraph in the text.

When students have completed the assignment, pair them up and have them compare summaries for similarities and differences. Ask the pairs of students to write a joint consensus summary. Discuss these in class.

This assignment should be done, on the average, about once a week throughout the school year.

● Provide students with a one-paragraph summary you have written for a possible newspaper article. Using the summary as a guide, have them write an article to fit. For example:

SUMMARY

This article is about a fire in an apartment building in the city. No one was injured, but the fire department is investigating the possibility of arson.

ARTICLE

Ellensburg, WA. The Ellensburg Fire Department responded to a fire in the Racy Arms Apartments at 1055 W. Elm early this morning. Three apartment units were destroyed and two badly damaged, although no one was injured.

Chief William Jenson indicated to the press that they had not yet determined the exact cause of the conflagration but would be having an investigation to see whether arson was involved.

(Note that the following activity is essentially designed to help students learn to paraphrase rather than summarize. However, the importance of paraphrasing in summarizing clearly warrants attention to this skill.)

● Have students assume the role of newspaper reporters. Ask them to take a popular fairy tale or folktale and write it in contemporary language as an article for the school paper or local newspaper. Provide something like the following as a model for them to use.

CINDERELLA WOWS PRINCE, THEN BOWS OUT!

TOOLEYS, OREGON—Last night was unique for the annual gala coming-out dance sponsored by the Tooleys J.C.s. A beautiful young woman stole the show from all others as she rocked the evening away with Prince Charming to the music of Danny Cagle and the Buckoo Beavers.

It was clear that her three stepsisters were not too happy, as they had to sit the evening out nibbling on carrot sticks and Swedish meatballs while the strobe lights did their best to help Cinderella and Prince Charming electrify the crowd with their latest rock steps.

A mystery does remain, however, since the beautiful young woman quickly left the scene just as the clock struck twelve. Leaving only a shoe she did not take the time to put back on after dancing, she astounded all, especially the Prince.

He would like to see her again and is offering a $1,000.00 reward to anyone who can provide information as to her whereabouts.

She was last seen roaring out of the parking lot in her dark-maroon Porsche 911 with Oregon license plates.

If you know of her whereabouts and would like to land a $1,000.00 reward from the Prince, give him a call at 503/721-8890.

Reciprocal Questioning

Within the past half-dozen years or more, a particular interest has developed in the use of reciprocal questioning to help readers develop metacognitive skills. Simply put, reciprocal questioning reverses the questioning process so that students ask the questions rather than answer them. Practitioners and other reading educators, including reading researchers, advocate incorporating this activity into the total reading program. Certainly one thing in favor of this is that students tend to like these kinds of activities. Think about it—it is one of the few times in reading class that they can ask questions rather than answer them!

Techniques and Activities

● Provide students with a sample of text or select one from a basal reader or other source of reading instruction material. Tell them to read the text silently (keep the text passage short enough to be read in five or six minutes). Tell them that after they have read the text you will ask them two questions to find out whether or not they understood what they read.

After they have done the reading, ask the two questions and discuss the responses from your students with the class.

Now ask them to silently read a different text or the next portion of the same text. This time, however, they are to write down two questions they can ask you to determine whether or not you understood what was in the text.

Notice how this activity requires your students to think about what they think about when trying to determine the meaning of a text!

You can vary this activity by having students write questions for each other or for the rest of the class. You can pair them up or put learners into small groups and ask them to select the best questions from the pair or group. Have them discuss why some questions are better than others.

Taxonomizing Questions

As noted in an earlier chapter, reading educators have agreed for some time that levels of questions vary, that students should learn to think at various levels, and that different levels of questions on the taxonomy can help in thinking and comprehension development. Most classroom teachers are familiar with one or more of the various question taxonomies available, e.g., Bloom, Sanders, Barrett, and others. Effective teachers of reading comprehension use some taxonomy in designing questioning strategies for instruction and when designing questions for testing and monitoring student growth in reading. For many of us the use of questioning taxonomies stops here; we have not thought further on the matter. Yet an excellent technique exists to help students' metacognitive development: Have your students taxonomize the questions. Here are some techniques and activities designed to help you do that at a variety of grade levels, from primary on up through secondary grades.

Techniques and Activities

• Take students through the following steps. As you read these steps, think about an appropriate modification of this model for your grade level. The example provided here is suited for third or fourth grade.

1. Provide the following or some other appropriate text for your students. Ask them to read it to themselves, or you read it to them.

ANTARCTICA

The land where the South Pole is located is called Antarctica. No one lives there except people doing research, because it is too cold there.

Because it is so cold, early explorers had to be very strong and courageous. Two important early explorers who went to Antarctica in the early twentieth century were Robert Scott and Roald Amundsen.

2. Ask your students the following questions:
    a. What is the land called where the South Pole is located?
    b. When did two early explorers go there?
    c. Name the two explorers who traveled there.

3. Ask students to justify their answers, i.e., How do you know? Most not only will indicate that the answers are in the text, but will point out the answers in the text for you. Encourage them to do this.

4. Now ask your students the following question: Do you think Robert Scott was frightened when he was in Antarctica?

5. Ask students to justify their answers. Discuss with them that the answer to this question cannot be found directly in the text.

    Indicate to your students that we call questions of the first kind, i.e., those whose answers can be found directly in the text—those where you can point out the answer with your finger if asked to— *fact questions*. Tell them that the questions whose answers cannot be found directly in the text or questions which require us to think before we can answer them are called *think questions*. Fact questions and think questions are two different kinds of important questions.

6. Provide students with the following questions, asking them to identify each as a fact question or as a think question.
    a. What is the temperature like in Antarctica? (Fact)
    b. Do any researchers live in Antarctica? (Fact)
    c. Would you like to go to Antarctica? (Think)

    Discuss with them why the first two are fact questions and the last one is a think question.

7. Provide students with examples of fact and think questions about a variety of topics and ask them to identify each. For example:
    a. When did Columbus discover America?
    b. How many ships did Columbus have in his fleet?
    c. Was Columbus frightened when he came to America?

    (Notice that without a context, a question like the last one could be either a fact or a think question. However, given the nature of the previous two questions, the wording at least would suggest a think question. This is what we want students to get used to looking at.)

8. Provide students with a short text and ask them to write two fact questions, based upon the text, and one think question.

9. Have students exchange their questions and see if each can categorize the other's questions according to this simplified taxonomy.

10. Discuss with them the differences and why both kinds of questions are important.

● With older students the taxonomy of question types can be increased to provide more sophistication to this technique. One of the easier and more straightforward of the popular question taxonomies is the Sanders taxonomy (Sanders, 1966).

Here is an overview of the Sanders taxonomy of questions:

1. All thinking can be classified into seven levels which have been named *memory, translation, interpretation, application, analysis, synthesis,* and *evaluation.*
2. These levels of questions are appropriate for all grade levels and all subjects.
3. Question level is determined by context and background experiences of the learner as well as by level definition.

Level 1: *Memory.* The learner is asked to recall or recognize ideas or facts presented directly in text. Example: When did Columbus discover America?

Level 2: *Translation.* The learner is asked to restate an idea in different language (paraphrase). Example: Tell me in your own words what this means.

Level 3: *Interpretation.* The learner is asked to compare certain ideas or use an idea that he or she studied previously. Example: In what range of temperature, rainfall, and topography is cotton grown in the United States? (Condition of question-asking: The students have studied temperature, rainfall, and topography maps of the United States.)

Level 4: *Application.* The learner is asked to apply a concept, skill, or principle learned earlier to a new situation without being told explicitly to do so. Example: Write a letter to Mr. Jones thanking him for showing us the dairy. (The teacher is actually testing students' ability to write complete sentences after a unit in language arts.)

Level 5: *Analysis.* The learner is expected to apply basic rules of formal reasoning, i.e., inductive or deductive reasoning, to solve a problem. Example: What is wrong with the statement, "Everybody likes golfing"?

Level 6: *Synthesis.* The learner is asked to create or generate something. Synthesis questions never have one correct response. Example: Write a poem about a star. (Note: This would *not* be a synthesis question if asked after studying a unit in poetry writing.)

Level 7: *Evaluation.* The learner is asked to judge the worth of some product, idea, or situation. Judgments themselves cannot be assessed as being right or wrong; however, the processes employed and justification provided can be critiqued in terms of their applicability. Example: Did the Colonists do the right thing in throwing the tea overboard at the Boston Tea Party?

A variety of taxonomy types are available, however. For example, in social studies, the following can be useful in helping students comprehend text couched in the unique language and structures of the social sciences.

I. *Identification.* Example: Who is it? Where did it take place? Can you define . . . ?

II. *Description.* Example: What are they doing? What did it look like? What happened?

III. *Comparative.* Example: How are they different? Alike? How is this event like X event? How is X analogous to Y?

IV. *Historical.* Example: How did X get started? What have they found to be true in the past? Which came first, X or Y? How do you know?

V. *Cause and Effect.* Example: Why did X happen? If Y happens, will X happen? How could X have been avoided?

VI. *Prediction.* Example: What will happen next? How will this end? What do you think will happen at the end of the war?

VII. *Creative.* Example: How would you have handled X? What would you do if . . . ? What do you think should be done if Y happens?

VIII. *Research.* Example: How can we find out? Which are the facts and which are the opinions? What evidence can you present?

IX. *Value Inquiry.* Example: Which way do you think is best? Was the author's solution to the crime a good one? How would you rewrite the end of the Civil War?

X. *Relevance or Application.* Example: How does this apply to me? What did we learn from World War II? How can we prevent another?

An example of a different kind of taxonomy that could be used in English classes is a *literary immersion level* taxonomy. The following is an example:

> Level 1: *Physical Plane Actions.* The learner is expected to know the specifics and details of plot, character, action, and so on. Example: When did Jim go to the beach?
>
> Level 2: *Explanatory/Justification Plane.* The learner is asked to explain or justify actions or events using knowledge of physical plane actions and appropriate reasoning. Example: Why did Jim decide to go to the beach when he did?
>
> Level 3: *Psychological/Sociological Implication Plane.* The learner is expected to know the social or psychological forces beyond the individual that shape the actions or events. Example: What basic social rule was Jim responding to when he went to the beach?
>
> Level 4: *Philosophical Plane.* The learner is expected to provide personal insight into the nature of man or of certain universal truths or beliefs that govern our behavior. Example: Was Jim doing what was right for a human being to do under these conditions when he went to the beach?

As you examine the various question taxonomies that have been offered over the past twenty years or so, you will see that they attempt to address different mental processes or different skills. Ability to categorize reality in a number of different ways is important. Ability to think about the different ways in which textual ideas, events, and developments can be categorized while reading the text is also important. That is why activities and techniques such as these possess potential for your classroom.

Writing Math Story Problems

Mathematics is one of the more difficult areas of study in which reading comprehension plays a critical role. Within this area, one of the most difficult things for students to handle is the *story problem*. Although part of the difficulty with story problems is the mathematics involved, there also appears to be difficulty in comprehending the structure of the language of the story problems as well. The following instructional activity can help students in this troublesome area.

Activity

● Provide each of your students with a separate set of math equations, e.g., $10.95 − $5.95 = $4.00. Ask them to write story problems for each of the math equations. Include one or two examples for your students. For example:

Math Equation: $10.95 − $5.95 = $4.00

Story Problem: Mary Ellen mowed her neighbor's lawn one day. She earned $10.95 for the job. She was now able to buy the pair of sports socks she had been wanting. They cost $5.95. How much money did she have left?

Have your students write their story problems without giving the answer; have them exchange their problems with a classmate. Ask each of the students to solve the story problems written by their friends.

Self-Interrupted Oral Reading

During their reading good readers carry on a conversation with themselves. We use *inner speech* to talk with ourselves as we read. In fact, that is how we self-monitor to assure that we are getting the essential information from the text.

Of course, while we read independently, no one, other than ourself, is privy to this conversation. Yet, as was indicated earlier in this book, this ability is critical for readers to develop. Unfortunately, most learners have never seen this self-with-self conversation take place. Modeling this practice for our students is one way to help them see what effective readers do during the act of reading.

Activity

● Prepare an overhead transparency with a paragraph or two from a novel, story, or nonfiction text. Choose one that you can relate to through prior experience or background knowledge, or one where there is particular challenge for unique reasons.

Read the text on the transparency to your class; attempt to voice your "self-monitoring" conversation. This is not particularly easy to do without some prior practice. For example:

Constable Green kept his expression as flat as the side of a slag heap and answered: "The Singer woman has lived in that cottage facing the Parade for nearly a year. No one in Lyme really knows her. She doesn't chat up the neighbors. She isn't friendly. She doesn't go out, except I've seen her sometimes at night, walking my beat. You might say she's eccentric."

Martha Grimes, Help the Poor Struggler

We shall asume that the reader of this excerpt has read the text up to this point and already knows the answers to many questions that a new reader would not know. We will skip those obvious questions, since the reader is supposed to be reflecting on only those that occur at the time this particular excerpt is read.

The reading from the transparency might go like this:

TEACHER READS ALOUD:	"Constable Green kept his expression flat . . ."
TEACHER SPEAKS ALOUD:	*Flat.* That's an interesting word. It makes sense here but is not a common descriptive word you meet every day.
TEACHER READS ALOUD:	". . . as the side of a slag heap . . . ."
TEACHER SPEAKS ALOUD:	I know about slag heaps for sure. I was raised in a coal-mining town in southern Illinois. Those slag heaps in Orient, where Uncle Mike and Aunt Emily lived; I remember those. Oh, oh. I'm digressing and losing track. I've got to get back to this plot.
TEACHER READS ALOUD:	". . . and answered: 'The Singer woman has lived in that cottage facing the Parade . . . .'"
TEACHER SPEAKS ALOUD:	Did the author talk about the Parade before? That's an odd expression. The word *the* used that way is really unusual. The street; the waterfront; the specific street area is what is meant here.
TEACHER READS ALOUD:	"'. . . for nearly a year. No one in Lyme really knows her. She doesn't chat up the neighbors.'"
TEACHER SPEAKS ALOUD:	"Doesn't chat up the neighbors." That is interesting. Strictly British. We'd never use that expression in the U.S. Means visit a lot.
TEACHER READS ALOUD:	"'She isn't friendly. She doesn't go out, except I've seen her sometimes at night, walking my beat.'"
TEACHER SPEAKS ALOUD:	The author is making her look too guilty here. I know that in mysteries you need characters to serve as straw people; they're not really guilty. They can't be. It's too obvious.
TEACHER READS ALOUD:	"'You might say she's eccentric.'"

During such an oral reading, students are likely to interject questions or comments. These can be incorporated in the demonstration.

Self-interruptions are excellent ways to model self-monitoring processes for your students. As your students become accustomed to this process, you can extend the text being read and encourage more discussion during your commentary.

With older students, you can expand the activity. Encourage students who are willing to model their own reading process aloud to the class from a text of their choice. Copies must be available to the class for maximum benefit from this activity.

You can vary the activity by giving students duplicate copies of a text. Ask them to write out their self-interrupted reading of the text. Discuss the difference in interruption points that occur with different readers. As you use this activity you will develop new ideas for its exploitation.

ADDITIONAL SELECTED READINGS

ESPY, W. (1975). *Words at play*. New York: Clarkson Potter.

HARRIS, T. and COOPER, E. (Eds.) (1985). *Reading, thinking, and concept development*. New York: College Entrance Examination Board.

KLEIN, M. (1985). *The development of writing in children: Pre-K through grade 8*. Englewood Cliffs, N.J.: Prentice-Hall.

KLEIN, M., LAMB, G. and WELCH, K. (1987). *Think and write: A reading workbook*. Boston: Ginn.

MOFFETT, J. and WAGNER, B. (1983). *A student-centerd language arts and reading curriculum: A handbook for teachers, grades K-13*. Boston: Houghton-Mifflin.

PAUK, W. (1974). *How to study in college*. Boston: Houghton-Mifflin.

VAUGHAN, J. and ESTES, T. (1986). *Reading and reasoning beyond the primary grades*. Newton, Mass.: Allyn & Bacon.

REFERENCES

BROWN, A. and DAY, J. D. (1983). Macrorules for summarizing texts: The development of expertise. Urbana, Ill.: Center for the Study of Reading, University of Illinois.

DAY, J. D. (1980). Teaching summarization skills: A comparison of training methods. Unpublished doctoral dissertation, University of Illinois.

GOUGH, P. (1984). Word recognition. In P. D. Pearson (Ed.), *Handbook of reading research*. New York: Longman.

KLEIN, M. (1973). Inferring from the conditional. Unpublished doctoral dissertation, University of Wisconsin.

MASON, J. (1984). When do children begin to read? An exploration of four-year-old children's letter- and word-reading competencies. *Reading Research Quarterly, 15*, 203-227.

SANDERS, N. (1966). *Classroom questions: What kinds?* New York: Harper & Row.

5

The Reading/Writing Connection

THE ROLE OF WRITING

Perhaps one of the most important contributions to improved reading comprehension in the past decade is the renewed emphasis upon writing, both as a fundamental aspect of our literacy and as an important language skill which can contribute directly to improved reading comprehension.

We have known for some time that there were correlations between reading achievement and writing ability. Loban documented these correlations in his classic longitudinal studies of the 1960s and 1970s (Loban, 1963; 1976). Stotsky reviewed and synthesized important experimental and correlational studies on the reading/writing connection (Stotsky, 1983) and also found that, essentially, those studies established strong relationships between the two language processes.

However, Stotsky's research review and synthesis suggested that certain limitations appeared in the relationship. For example, the use of writing generally appears to contribute more actively to improved reading than does the reverse. Reading programs, no matter how effective for improved reading comprehension, contribute little to improved writing skills, unless writing is a component of them.

One of the more intriguing points to surface from the majority of this research is that the relationship between reading and writing is a narrow, if rich, one. For example, simply providing your students with a wide array of writing opportunities in and of themselves will probably improve neither their reading nor their writing. Learning to write and learning to read are essentially that—*learned*; and, in the case of our society at least, they appear to be learned most effectively when they are taught.

That is, we know that good writers tend to be people who write more than poorer writers. We know, further, that fluency in writing comes when the writer has been given ample opportunity and solid encouragement, an encouraging and creative writing environment, and a supportive audience interested in what the writer has to say. We know, too, that fluency in writing is the first essential step in the process of learning to write. However, if students needed no more than the above factors present, then we would need only caring and understanding parents or caretakers to enable them to effectively produce the written language: We would not need teachers. However, we know that fluency—as essential as it is to the foundation of writing development—is the language and information source that the teacher uses to further direct instruction in writing.

There is some correspondence, too, with what takes place with reading development. We know that good readers read more often and read more effectively than do poorer readers. We know, too, that good readers tend to come from environments rich in literacy, with ample reading materials of various types. More fluent readers also possess larger and more usable vocabularies; as readers become more fluent, they become more avid and thus better readers. Fluency and practice tend to reinforce each other. Motivation is critical for developing fluency in both reading and writing. Some motivation can be planned in advance; some arises from the teaching context and the effective teacher, who capitalizes upon the moment.

However, if our students are going to benefit from a program that builds on the reading/writing relationship, we must remember a few things:

1. Fluency is an important goal for both reading and writing achievement. That means that **the classroom environment must be rich in literacy materials and that writing must take place on a consistent and regular basis.**

2. Teachers must capitalize upon the moment to incorporate writing in the reading program. While advance planning for the use of writing in the reading program is always necessary, the teacher must also be prepared to capitalize upon unique opportunities that arise.

3. Teachers and students must view the concept of *writing* as very comprehensive. To write doesn't mean just the act of creating an essay, preparing a report, composing a poem, or writing a short story: Teacher and students most perceive that **any act of written composition is writing**—an essay, a paragraph, a sentence, or even a single word.

Many, perhaps most, of the opportunities to use writing to improve reading comprehension arise in contexts not conducive to the development of full-blown essays or compositions of significant length. More often than not our *best* opportunities come with the conception of writing that includes virtually all times when pen or pencil and paper are put together by the composer.

4. The teacher must make a clear distinction between *writing-as-supplement* and *writing-as-integral* to the reading instruction! The best and most effective reading programs that incorporate writing are those which see a clear difference between these two notions.

Writing a poem or report prior to the reading lesson can be an important motivational technique. It can also provide additional background knowledge for the student. To some extent the same is true for writing activities after a text has been read; the subject can be studied further. Poetry, plays, or short stories can be written where the student uses the previously read text as a model or as an incentive for the writing.

While both these activities and techniques support the reading program, they fall into the category of writing-as-supplement to the reading. They do not contribute as substantively to the development of *specific* reading skills when done alone as do those activities and techniques which are designed from a writing-as-integral perspective. Teachers need to be able to do both, know when they are doing which, and know why and how they are going to do each.

ESTABLISHING THE MENTAL SET

How do you treat your personal books, the ones that are your favorites in your home and professional library? Certainly you take care of them, but what do you do with them while you are reading, or what have you done with them at some time in the past when you read them for the first time?

If you are like most readers, you keep a pen or pencil handy. You make checks or marks next to passages or particular words or sentences. You underline parts of text or use highlighter marking pens. Some get quite sophisticated, using a variety of colors to represent different categories of highlighted text. For me, blue or black is used to identify key information or important concepts I want to remember. This color combination is used most often in nonfiction and professional text where particular content and ideas are important enough for me to want to be able to refer back to them. Green is used to highlight sentences or larger units of text where I think the author has done a particularly effective job of using sentence or paragraph structure to make a point or paint a picture. This is found in both fiction and nonfiction but more predominantly in fiction. Favorite authors, such as William Styron, whom I regard as a superb stylist, get lots of green ink. Red is reserved for text that I find confusing or troublesome for some reason (either I do not understand it or I do not follow the author). Comments are written in the margins using all colors, depending on what I want to say.

Sometimes we turn down page corners—in spite of what our school librarians taught us through all of those school years! And, as noted, many of us keep a pen to write in the margins of our books. Sometimes we simply write notes to ourselves, sometimes we try to summarize key ideas in very brief fashion, sometimes we carry on a conversation with the author or argue with the author.

Notice how some of these practices qualify as *integrating-writing-into-reading*.

We have learned over the years that reading is an *active* process and not a *passive* one. The reader generates meaning rather than absorbs meaning from print. The reader *interacts* during the reading: interacts with self, interacts with the author, and interacts with the author's language. *These activities are necessary to generate meaning while reading a text.*

Given the usefulness of the above practices, it probably makes sense to encourage our students to do the same things with the books that they read. Publishers of basal readers and subject area textbooks, in particular, would like this policy, not to mention the dozens of publishers of the tradebooks that make their way into our classrooms and school libraries! Unfortunately, the financial circumstances of our public education system preclude advocating this practice.

However, there are two things teachers *can* do. First, encourage students to mark up books that they own. Encourage parents, relatives, and friends of students to purchase as gifts books in which your students can write.

Second (and perhaps more realistic), have students keep writing materials with them at all times during reading—whether during an actual reading class or any time they read, in the classroom and out. Spiral-bound notebooks work best because they can be used as journals without pages getting lost, they can be organized into different sections for different purposes, and so on.

The journal allows readers to maintain an ongoing conversation with themselves during the act of reading, to interact with the author of the text, and to make running commentary on the structure of the author's language and style. The journal also allows the teacher to monitor selected aspects of the readers' progress and provides an excellent opportunity for ongoing written dialogue with students about their reading and their responses to it.

We want students to view reading and writing as interactive parts of the same process. We want them to feel that pen and paper are as much a part of a reading lesson or reading a book as the book itself.

There is perhaps no better or more effective way for teachers to help students begin to connect these two close literacy domains than by example. Keep your notebook and pen with you as you read. If your school practices sustained silent reading, that is an excellent time to demonstrate the practice. Regardless, there are a number of opportunities that occur every day when the practice can be modeled for students—at all ages and in all grades.

Fluency has its roots in everyday application and use. Improving instruction in reading comprehension by employing writing requires a positive mental set on the part of the teacher that incorporates writing in all aspects of the reading program. Note, too, that the above uses establish the necessary mental set in your students.

Once this mental set is established, it is much easier to think of more expansive, elaborate ways to use writing in the reading program. Consider, for example, most of the questioning techniques and activities elaborated in Chapter 2. Many of these could incorporate writing as well as oral discourse, where *writing-as-integral* is the governing mode.

A positive writing-as-integral mental set means a better reading program.

Developing Prediction Skills Through Writing

● Provide students with a brief overview of a story they will be reading. Do not give them any details about the plot or character development.

For example, "You are going to read a story about a boy named Jimmy who lives on a farm. Jimmy decides to go fishing one day at a small pond. Before reading the story, think of some important words that might be in the story. Words like *water* and *fish*, for example. Write them down in a list."

After the students have prepared their lists of words, ask them to make up sentences and write the words in sentences related to the story. Then provide some specific questions requiring them to think about what might take place in the story. Again, encourage them to use the words they have in their list, but do not require it. For example:

1. Write a sentence that tells what Jimmy might do before he goes to the pond.
2. Write a sentence that tells what Jimmy might see at the pond.
3. Write two sentences that tell what Jimmy might do at the pond.
4. Write a sentence describing the most exciting thing that might happen to Jimmy at the pond.

After they have completed this series of tasks, provide them with a copy of the text and ask them to circle any of the words on their list that they find in the story.

Finally, have them write a brief paragraph indicating the biggest surprise for them in the story, i.e., what was there in the story that they didn't expect to find there. You could use a number of alternative assignments in this last step which would enable them to tie the story to the projections they had made prior to the reading.

This activity can be modified for different grade levels and subject areas. It can also be refined to fit into the predict-test-conclude questioning strategy presented in Chapter 2.

● Select a short text, e.g., brief newspaper article, selection from subject area textbook or basal reader, and pull out several important points made in the article. Organize these into a list of statements or facts, including enough information for students to get the gist of the text easily. For example:

1. Thomas Leffingwell searched for buried treasure on his property much of his life.
2. He died without finding it.
3. Workers found over $10,000 worth of coins and art in a secret room of the house.
4. His wife, Ann, said that this was not the treasure he searched for.
5. There were 200 coins in an 1856 Mason jar and a wine decanter.
6. Two of the coins were worth an estimated $650 apiece.
7. Another prize was a Half Anna, issued in 1855 by the East India Company.
8. The collection also included Indian-head coins, women's rights currency, and a paper called a freedman's currency.

Give this information to your students and ask them to use it to prepare a newspaper article with these statements serving as the essential data source. They will need to add some things and reword most of the statements.

Give them the actual article after they have finished writing theirs.

TREASURE CHEST FOUND IN HOUSE'S SECRET ROOM

Aurora, N.Y.—For almost 80 years, Thomas Leffingwell wondered if his father's tale of buried treasure was true. He searched all his life, but he went to his grave without finding the truth.

This week, 12 years after Leffingwell died, two workmen at his home stumbled upon a secret room and found a hidden cache of at least $10,000 in old coins and a booty of 19th century toys.

Ann Lawrence, who was married to Leffingwell, said Tuesday that the find probably isn't the treasure his father told him about, because it was said to have been buried under a tree.

For years, Leffingwell had dug holes all around the yard of the 140-year-old house overlooking Cayuga Lake in upstate New York, even hiring workmen to do it for him. But he found nothing.

Workmen John Van Nostrand and Sean Nolan found the secret room and its contents over the weekend, on the very day Lawrence had told them of her former husband's story about hidden treasure.

What they found are an 1856 Mason jar and a cork-lined wine decanter containing more than 200 coins, most in good condition, dating from 1803 to the 1860's. Two 3-cent coins dated 1869 are worth an estimated $650 apiece.

Another prize was a coin called a Half Anna, issued in 1855 by the East India Co., a British mercantile operation that ran like an independent fiefdom.

Indian-head coins, women's rights currency 1879 and a piece of paper called a freedman's currency, carrying the likeness of a freed slave, complete the collection.

The Bellingham Herald,
Wed., August 27, 1986

After students have compared their own drafts with the actual article, you have several options—pair students for comparison of their versions, discuss the article in class, use the article to generate additional writing, and so on.

You can vary the difficulty of this activity by controlling the kind and quantity of information given to the students to prepare their articles.

Paraphrasing and Summarizing

Although both paraphrase and summary can be oral and written, the written approach is clearly the most effective. Writing paraphrases and summaries during the reading allow the reader to actively pursue the reading process as one that generates meaning.

Paraphrase and summary writing during the postreading phase allow the student to substantiate specific information acquired for both short-term and long-term memory. In addition, summarizing especially provides the teacher with what is probably the best single means for monitoring student progress in reading comprehension.

A number of skills underlie both paraphrasing and summarizing. The ability to paraphrase correlates directly with vocabulary range. Knowledge of synonyms, antonyms, and so on, and the abilities to reason analogically, to see metaphoric relationships, and to understand the difference between literal and metaphoric statements or thoughts are all important to paraphrasing. Therefore, many of the activities used in good reading programs not only increase reading vocabulary but also provide essential background and skills for the student to make effective use of the vocabulary.

The abilities to classify, seriate (sequence), determine cause-effect relationships, locate main-idea statements, delete extraneous material or information, view ideas globally, and relate generalizations to particular assertions are among the foundation skills necessary for a reader to summarize effectively.

To have the strongest paraphrasing and summarizing components in a reading program then, our students must have already developed the critical foundation skills for these activities. If that is what we want, it is clear that reading programs in the early grades must build these foundation skills.

In addition, continued work in the foundation skills should take place throughout the grades, with increased sophistication and refinement. For example, classification and seriation activities should become more complex and subtle. Traditionally, in the early grades most seriation has been by size, volume, or numerical order. More demanding seriation can incorporate sequencing by importance or by aesthetic appeal, requiring the learner to provide justification for the order selected. Classification categories can be expanded or shrunk, or subject matter can be varied according to level or degree of difficulty.

Increasingly, as the student progresses through the grades, foundation-skill activities should be incorporated into direct paraphrasing and summarizing activities. Examples of such activities follow.

Paraphrasing Activities

● Provide students with famous quotes and ask them to restate the quote. For example:

"A rose by any other name . . . ." (Shakespeare)

Restatement:
No matter what appellation is applied, the physical characteristics do not vary.
Or,
A floribunda from any other lineage would present nearly the same degree of aromatic pleasure.
Or,
A rose endowed with an alternative nomenclature would exude an aroma as fragrant.
Or,
If a bloom from the division Magnoliophyta, family Rosaceae were to be reclassified with another appellation, its redolence would remain relatively unchanged.

"The world likes humor, but it treats it patronizingly." (E.B. White)

Restatement:

People like to have fun but don't take it seriously.

Or,

It's OK to have a laugh on occasion, just don't get carried away.

● Provide students with one form of text and ask them to rewrite it retaining as much of the original meaning as possible. For example, have them write a poem as an essay or an essay as a poem; have them convert a short story into a play or a play into a short story. Activities such as these can be followed effectively by discussion of the strengths and limitations of the rewrites. What is gained or lost by paraphrasing in a different literary form?

● Modified drama writing is especially effective in subject areas where there is an issue or issues related to the text assignment. For example, the issue of states rights versus federal government rights in the founding days of our nation represents an excellent opportunity. Have students write the dialogue that might take place if Alexander Hamilton, a strong federal government advocate, were to bump into Thomas Jefferson, a strong states advocate, while on a stroll in a park.

During a postreading, such an activity provides the basis for considerable class discussion of the various interpretations the students have made of ideas or statements expressed by famous people.

Summarizing Activities

● Prepare handouts from a basal reader or subject area textbook. After each paragraph, type in lines where students can write a one-sentence summary for each paragraph. Vary the length of the text to fit the grade or developmental level of your students, which you can change as they become more proficient or to challenge them. Remember to use different forms of text, i.e., fiction and nonfiction. Also, this format can be varied to present larger chunks of text to the reader, e.g., three or four paragraphs, and then several lines for them to write brief paragraph summaries of the larger units of discourse they have read.

Your students should do this activity *during* the reading of the text, although the results of their writing can provide excellent resources for follow-up discussions during postreading.

Keep these handouts on file. Over time you will find that your selection will grow, allowing a wider variety of timely and appropriate text for various occasions.

● Use inserted questions in text handouts which focus on summarizing ideas or specifics in content. Provide appropriate lines for students to write on *during* their reading. Again, these written summaries should make excellent resources for class or small-group discussion during postreading.

Journal Writing

Journal writing has long been a favorite mainstay of good composition programs throughout the grades. The advantages are many and most are fairly obvious. Journal writing is probably the most personal writing possible in a school setting. The journal can be either public, private, or both. Traditionally, it has been at least semi-public in character, with the student sharing much of the writing with the teacher and other students in the class.

Journals represent the best single opportunity for students to write daily. The writer can relate elements of a narrative in a meaningful fashion. Because the journal has this advantage, it, perhaps more than any other device in composition instruction, can contribute to the development of fluency in the writer—the most critical first characteristic of better writers.

Since the journal is easily accessible, it allows the teacher to incorporate last-minute writing into a variety of lessons or contexts. It is also an excellent way for the teacher to monitor student growth—not only in writing, but in subject areas as well.

The potential of the journal as a primary part of the reading program, however, has yet to be fully developed. If one buys into the notion of writing-as-integral to the reading program and crucial to the development of effective reading comprehension, then the journal is probably the best single resource to incorporate writing into reading instruction. The reader-as-writer and the writer-as-reader are two sides of the same coin. Whether or not reading and writing use the same mental processes (they may or may not, depending upon how precisely we define *mental processing*), they work closely with the same data sources—language and thought. There is simply too much research to support the connection of the two to think otherwise.

To help students develop and maintain the writer-as-reader/reader-as-writer concept, early writing must be encouraged (Harste et al., 1984; Graves, 1983; and others). During the preschool and earliest school years, this will mean *scribble writing*, later use of pictographs, and finally conversion to the ideographs which are used in our written language. Throughout the school years, it also means a necessary *fluency* in writing. To a significant extent, children learn to write by writing; that writing must be encouraged and expected on a daily basis for a variety of purposes and a variety of audiences (Klein, 1985).

The journal serves not only as a general tool for the development of fluency, but when used effectively, also as the *single* most effective tool for bringing the writer-as-reader and the reader-as-writer into consonance. Used effectively, **the journal represents the best single instructional**

opportunity available to the teacher **for making writing an integral and ongoing part** of reading comprehension instruction.

Before considering activities and techniques to incorporate journal writing into reading instruction, we should note the following guidelines:

1. From first grade on, all students should have a journal available at all times in the classroom.

2. Students should always have some time for private writing in their journals, writing that they share with no one *unless* they choose to do so. This often requires that they have more than one notebook, to ensure privacy. Most writing is done with an audience in mind; and generally, as teachers who have used journals know, most children, especially the younger ones, prefer to share it. However, there should be an option for at least some journal writing to be private.

3. Students should learn through their classroom experience that the journal is part of their reading instruction. During reading class specifically, the journal is out and ready for writing. The same is true during classes in content areas such as social studies and science. Writing materials are as much a part of the act of reading as are books and other forms of text.

4. As a teacher, you should maintain your own journal, and at least some time each day you and your class should write in your journals. Effective teachers of reading who use a writing-as-integral approach must be practitioners of the craft of writing themselves. It is difficult to appreciate the challenge, beauty, and relevance of writing to reading without engaging in the process yourself on a regular basis.

5. Students should be encouraged to use the journal at all times when reading, including outside of class. Library and personal books should be read with pen or pencil in hand and journal ready for use.

6. Finally, the teacher's ultimate goal is achieved when students choose to write in their journals to maintain an ongoing conversation with themselves about their reading. That means that teacher-directed instruction in the use of writing is, in some sense, simply a step in the direction of student-chosen writing for personally chosen motives.

The activities and techniques that follow will hopefully move the student toward that long-range goal of using writing because it is a natural part of the reading process.

Journal Dialoguing

Basically, journal dialoguing is conversation between student and teacher written in the student's journal. To do this, the student portions off a section of the journal and divides each page in half vertically with a line. The student writes in the left-hand column of each page.

The student can make entries in this section daily or less often (perhaps twice a week). The teacher then collects the journal from the student and writes comments or questions in the right-hand column.

Several benefits accrue from this technique. It gives the teacher the chance to probe into a student's reading physically as well as mentally. If students have difficulty with particular forms of texts or text structures, or have particular likes or dislikes in reading topics, or have difficulty applying particular skills in reading comprehension, as well as a number of other specifics, such problems can often be spotted in the journal dialoguing.

Journal dialoguing is also effective for teaching students how to think through a text when there appear to be self-monitoring difficulties or metacognitive problems in dealing with it.

Following is an example of journal dialoguing with a student over a period of several days in which the teacher, through probing questions, helps the student think through his reading more effectively. Along the way, the student develops greater facility in expressing ideas related directly to comprehension of the text.

STUDENT COMMENTS	TEACHER COMMENTS
I just read this story called "The Cat Who Became a Poet" and I think it's a dumb story!	Why do you say that? You must have some reasons.
Oh, I don't know. It's just that nobody ever heard of a mouse that was a poet or a cat that talked in poetry talk.	What do you mean by *poetry talk*?
Well, the cat couldn't meow but when he would open his mouth to meow he would say poetry instead after he had eaten the mouse that was a poet.	Oh, I see. And you think that it wasn't very believeable for a cat to be doing that?
No.	Do you think it important that everything in all stories be believable?
Well, some things can be made up but most of the stuff ought to be real like.	Why do you suppose the author used this nonreal poetry-reading cat in this story?
I guess she was trying to make some kind of point.	Like what?
Well, the cat was able to get away from the dog because he knew poetry and could do other things that cats couldn't do. Maybe that was it.	I think you're right, Jim. Maybe the cat also learned something about his own behavior as well.
You got that right. He probably won't go around eating mice so much anymore!	

Opportunities to monitor student growth in both reading and writing are excellent when journal dialoguing with students involves their reading, also.

Regardless of use, remember that, like any good teaching technique, journal dialoguing can be overdone and thus lose its effectiveness. Normally, you can sense when students feel that they are devoting more time than necessary to it. To reap full benefit though, it must be used selectively but predictably throughout the school year.

Sections Within the Journal

• Have students section off part of their journal for separate entries about their outside reading. Use a simple format calling for title and author, followed by a short paragraph or two—one paragraph briefly summarizing the text read; one paragraph telling why the student liked or disliked the selection.

These sections can be read by other students interested in reading the same text. The writing then becomes an excellent resource for class discussion of supplementary readings.

• Have students keep a section of their journal for new reading vocabulary. They should get in the habit of identifying a word and using it in a sentence relevant to the selection they found the word in, perhaps even the same sentence in which the word first appeared.

• Have students keep a section of the journal for summarizing and paraphrasing activities from assigned texts. Be sure they have a system that allows them to refer to the summaries later for review, e.g., entries by topic, theme, text type, date, and so on.

Developing Point of View Through Writing

Comprehending an author's point of view can be difficult, even for good readers. As a literary concept, it is quite demanding. Normally, the author uses a variety of techniques to achieve a particular point of view. However, the literary form chosen plays some part. Poetry, for example, dictates a specific and somewhat limited range of viewpoints. In addition to form, topic, sentence structure, vocabulary, setting, and so on all work to shape point of view. By writing themselves, students become sensitized to the techniques available to the author and the importance of considering the reader when taking a particular point of view in writing.

The following are helpful in accomplishing this.

Techniques and Activities

To teach your students to establish psychological distance between author and audience, have them pretend that they went camping in the mountains (actually taking them, with accompanying notebooks, is better, of course). In the middle of the night, a bear rambles into the camp, messes around with the food and cooking utensils, and generally causes a ruckus, although no one is injured. Eventually the bear is frightened off. (You can also give your students an actual nonfiction text that describes such an event.)

Jot down notes of things you would like to remember about the incident. Since no one will be reading these notes but yourself, you need not take the care you normally would if you were writing for someone else.

Have your students do the same. Let them keep their notes, or else collect them and hold onto them yourself.

After a few days, return the notes. Have your students use them to write a letter to a close friend or relative to tell them about the event. Again, keep the notes or have the students do so.

Several days later, tell your students that the local newspaper has heard about the great "Bear Scare" and wants to run a feature story about it. Have them use their notes to prepare a brief newspaper article suitable for publication in the local paper.

Notice how the student has to increase the psychological distance between self and audience with each of the subsequent writing tasks.

Follow this by examining samples of various texts written with different audiences in mind. Discuss the salient features of each and how the author communicates with each audience.

● Identify some issues in the news or locally. Present a brief, written text (one or two paragraphs) elaborating a particular point of view, followed by a similar text on the same topic but from an opposite point of view. Then present your students with a new text that reflects a given point of view and have them write the opposite point of view using your example as a model. For example:

Point of View:

>The Senator said that the farming bill was necessary. Farmers were in financial trouble and needed support. It was the responsibility of the government to see that they were accorded their fair share. They shouldn't have to work for nothing. Farming was the backbone of American society.

Opposite point of view:

>The Senator said that the farming bill was unnecessary. Farmers were overpaid and needed no help. It was the responsibility of the individual to see that he carried his own weight. The government shouldn't have to provide everything. Farmers had always been a drain on American society.

Now read this sample text reflecting a specific point of view:

>The poor in the United States are in the worst economic and social situation they have been in since the founding of the country. The percentage of families falling below the poverty level increases every year. Social programs designed to provide assistance have been elimi-

nated or cut back drastically. This is wrong. The nation has an obligation to support the needy. We need new legislation and strong budget
support now!

Write a paragraph with an opposing point of view to this one.

After students have prepared their point-of-view paragraphs, discuss
the strengths and limitations of the models provided. Have students work
in pairs or small groups to identify the kind of information lacking from
both the model paragraphs and their own. Discuss in class how authors
develop point of view with selective use of information. Use examples from
texts used in class.

Although the techniques and activities presented in this chapter are
selective, they do represent examples from which a broader and richer
array of selections can be made. They are intended to fall across the entire
reading instruction phase range—prereading, reading, and postreading.
Used selectively and appropriately on a consistent basis and in a teaching
environment committed to the concept of writing-as-integral to improved
reading comprehension, these techniques and activities should do their
part to improve your reading program.

ADDITIONAL SELECTED READINGS

HENNINGS, D. (1982). A writing approach to reading comprehension—Schema theory in
action. *Language Arts, 59 (1),* 8-17.

IRWIN, J. W. (1986). *Teaching reading comprehension processes.* Englewood Cliffs, N.J.: Prentice-
Hall.

KLEIN, M. (1985). *The development of writing in children: Pre-K through grade eight.* Englewood
Cliffs, N.J.: Prentice-Hall.

McCRACKEN, M. and McCRACKEN, R. (1979). *Reading, writing and language: A practical guide
for primary teachers.* Winnepeg: Penguin Publishers.

MOFFETT, J. and WAGNER, B. (1983). *Student-centered language arts and reading, K-12.* Boston:
Houghton-Mifflin.

MOSENTHAL, P. TAMOR, L. and WALMSLEY, S. (Eds.). (1983). *Research on writing: Principles
and methods.* New York: Longman.

RUBIN, A. and BRUCE, B. (1984). QUILL: Reading and writing with a microcomputer. In
B.A. Hutson (Ed.), *Advances in reading and language research.* Greenwich, Conn.: JAI
Press.

RUBIN, A. and HANSEN, J. (1985). Reading and writing: How are the first two "R's" related?
In J. Orasanu (Ed.), *A decade of reading research: Implications for practice.* Hillsdale, N.J.:
Erlbaum.

TEALE, W. and SULZBY, E. (Eds.). *Emergent literacy: Writing and reading.* Norwood, N.J.: Ablex.

REFERENCES

HARSTE, J., WOODWARD, V. and BURKE, C. (1984). *Language stories and literacy lessons.* Portsmouth, N.H.: Heinemann Educational Books.

GRAVES, D. (1983). *Writing.* Portsmouth, N.H.: Heinemann Educational Books.

KLEIN, M. (1985). *The development of writing in children: Pre-K through grade eight.* Englewood
Cliffs, N.J.: Prentice-Hall.

LOBAN, W. (1976). *Language development: Kindergarten through grade 12.* Champaign, Ill.: NCTE.

LOBAN, W. (1963). *The language of elementary school children.* Champaign, Ill.: NCTE.

STOTSKY, S. (1983). Research on reading/writing relationships: A synthesis and suggested directions. *Language Arts, 60,* 627-642.

Teaching Text Structure and Organization

TEXT STRUCTURES

This chapter focuses upon the structure and organization of text, its forms and types, and how it is generated and built. In contrast to earlier chapters, here we are more concerned with the structure and logic of the language used in the text than we are with the reader and how he or she generates meaning.

All-around effective readers must not only know how to use a variety of strategies and processes to generate meaning for text, but also must be prepared to address a variety of text types and forms. They must realize that different kinds of text are organized differently and that the language of different forms of text tends to be structured differently.

For example, two of the most predominant forms of text that the typical reader meets are exposition and narration. Exposition describes or elaborates events, activities, or ideas in a relatively objective fashion. Typically, its organization is straightforward; it includes a stated main-idea topic sentence or an oblique thesis assertion with the main idea borne by the structure of the paragraph or longer discourse unit. Exposition employs stylistic devices such as sequencing by importance, explanation by definition (including a number of defining types and styles), arrangement of supporting detail by relation to the thesis, and the use of compare-and-contrast with selected subjects.

Expository text is essentially nonfiction in character, i.e., the type of text found on the front pages of newspapers, in essays and reports, or in book reviews. It is the type of text that freshmen in college are usually asked to write in the introductory composition class. It dominates most content area textbooks, while it makes up only a minority of the text in most basal reading programs.

Essentially, narrative text is subjective description and elaboration. Its organization is not necessarily straightforward; in fact, the organization is largely semantic with more or less detailed description in each sentence relative to that which precedes or which follows. In narration, it is easier to track the level of abstraction movement than to organize it as you would an expository text.

If we wish our students to be the most effective readers possible, then we must include direct instruction in text structures in our reading program. Students should know the basic differences between narration and exposition, for example, along with other elements of text structure and organization. The remainder of this chapter discusses these areas.

BUILDING SENTENCES

Regardless of text type or form, the sentence is the most important fundamental meaning-bearing unit beyond the word. In fact, it is reasonable to think in terms of *sentence meanings* as well as *word meanings*. For example, imagine that in the following three contexts, a child utters the same two words, but with different intonation and emphasis.

1. "Mommy car!" (Child telling another that this particular vehicle belongs to her mother.)
2. "Mommy car!" (Child telling her mother that she spots a vehicle approaching on the street.)
3. "Mommy car." (Child indicating to her mother that she wishes to accompany her in the family vehicle.)

One important thing that we have learned about sentences and their structure over the past three decades or so is that they are not created by simply attaching one word to another and ending that string with a period. Sentences are, instead, built; generated from a smaller set of structural patterns by applying a fixed set of *change* or *transformation rules* to the smaller set to generate more complex sentences. For example, consider this sentence:

The bright young girl studied the new teacher.

This sentence is built from four smaller sentences:

1. The girl is bright.
2. The girl is young.
3. The girl studied the teacher.
4. The teacher is new.

Sentence three is the foundation, or *consumer*, sentence since it contains the basic verb phrase crucial to the final sentence. Sentences one, two, and four are all altered by applying a *modification reduction rule* which makes a noun phrase of each. Sentences one and two are then combined and placed in front of the foundation sentence to create the subject. After the rule application, Sentence four is placed after the verb to become the direct object in the final sentence.

We operate with two sets of rules in our head which we use either to produce or analyze sentences. The first set, called *generative rules*, allows us to produce simplified sentences, similar in structural complexity to those found in most primers and beginning readers in basal reading programs. (Notice that structural similarity and semantic similarity need not be the same thing.) Meaning generated in our heads is often initially manifested in these kinds of sentences.Children up through seven years of age or so rely heavily upon this first set of generative rules for producing spoken and written sentences.

As children mature, they begin to apply a second set of rules, called *transformation rules*. These rules operate upon the simple sentences produced by our generative rule set. They work to change the simpler sentences, move them around, combine them, and so on to result in the more elegant and sophisticated sentences found in more mature text.

Transformation rules alter the simple-sentence set in one or more of four ways:

1. Addition, i.e., $X + Y \rightarrow X + Y + Z$
2. Deletion, i.e., $X + Y \rightarrow X$ or Y
3. Embedding, i.e., $X + Y \rightarrow X + Z + Y$
4. Permutation, i.e., $X + Y \rightarrow Y + X$

These rules allow us to produce and comprehend more complex sentences containing modification, coordination, predication, and subordination—the grammatical structures used to both clarify *and* complicate text structure.

In summary, generative rules produce simple sentences devoid of significant modification, subordination, or coordination. But when you see sentences with adjectives, subordinating conjunctions (*since, because, although, whenever, if-then,* and so on), relative pronouns (*who, which, that*), or coordinating conjunctions (*and, but, or;* and *for,* in limited contexts), you know that transformation rules have produced the sentence.

To read effectively, do readers have to be taught the specific, formal sets of rules? No. To write well, do authors have to be taught these rules? No.

Do developing readers need to know anything about these rules and how to consciously apply them? Yes.

Readers need to know that:

1. Sentences are *built* in blocks or chunks of meaning from smaller units. Sentences are created *not* by adding one word to another, but by conceptualizing meaning in syntactic or grammatical constructs that can be bound together by application of our language-generating rules.
2. There is some relationship between text type and sentence structures generated by authors to fit that type, e.g., greater degree of modification in narrative text; greater degree of subordination in expository text; greater degree of coordination and parallelism in poetic text.
3. Conscious use of any knowledge, including grammatical knowledge, is better than unconscious use of such knowledge. We all know how to generate various kinds of sentences using the language-generating rules that we all possess. Readers and writers of greater facility simply expand their repertoire of syntactic choices by making more conscious use of their language-producing and language-consuming rules than do lesser readers and writers.

Teachers can engage students in techniques and activities designed to give them greater command of these rules.

Sentence-Combining

Activities that help readers apply sentence-generating rules help improve sentence comprehension (Combs, 1977; and others). Sentence-combining is the most useful of these activities. In simplest terms, sentence-combining takes a series of short, choppy sentences and combines them into one sentence.

For example:

The bug crawled down the rope.
The bug was tiny.
The rope was long.
The rope was rotten.

becomes:

The tiny bug crawled down the long, rotten rope.

We delete some words to avoid repetition, change the form of others in some instances, and on occasion add new words in the production of the new sentence.

Notice that each of the individual, short sentences represents a construction generated by our first set of grammatical rules. We apply our second set as we explore ways to combine them to yield our final sentence. We consciously apply rules we normally use unconsciously.

There are several types of sentence-combining activities:

Open-ended combining   This allows you to combine short sentences in any convenient and proper way. The above examples are open-ended. Students can develop alternative responses that are equally correct grammatically, although not necessarily equally pleasing rhetorically. Typically, open-ended sentence-combining generates various modifications. For example:

> The rain fell on the street.
> The rain was slow.
> The rain was chilly.
> The street was narrow.
> The street was old.

> Result: The slow chilly rain fell on the old narrow street. An alternative: On the old narrow street fell the slow chilly rain.

Some discussion could take place regarding the most rhetorically desirable of the two, although both are grammatical.

Cued combining   This gives the reader a consumer sentence followed by a cue word in parentheses. For example:

> The boy hit the ball. (who)
> The boy was big.
> The boy was my cousin.

> Result: The big boy who hit the ball was my cousin.

Cued sentence-combining can be used selectively to implicitly pressure the reader/writer to use practical grammatical constructs, in this case a relative clause introduced with the relative pronoun *who*.

Slotted combining   This uses a blank space, often filled with a place holder such as *someone* or *something*, in the consumer sentence. Changes made to other sentences are then done in such a way as to end up with a grammatical construct suitable for the slot position. For example:

> I know *something*.
> Joe is the leader. (that)

> Result: I know *that Joe is the leader.*

Here we have used a cue word in combination with the slot. Slotted sentence-combining, like cued, is more structured than is open-ended combining and can be used to teach specific grammatical constructs more directly.

Activities

• Select a good descriptive sentence in the first two-to-four pages of a story you are going to teach. Preferably, the sentence should either relate directly to the main idea or provide some insight into the main character or a key character.

Break the sentence down into its insert sentences—the short, choppy sentences from which it was built. You need not be absolutely accurate in this breakdown. Give these short sentences to your students in a handout before they read the story.

Ask your students to combine the sentences (we assume that they have had at least some sentence-combining experience prior to this activity). After they have done so, tell them that the sentence they just created, or one very close to it, can be found between page x and page y in the story. Ask them to find it.

After they have found the sentence, discuss how the students' sentences varied from the author's. This can be done as a class discussion or by pairs of students. Talk through the reasons for the differences. Use this opportunity to talk about the story. (Consider this activity as part of the overall questioning strategy you are using.)

Notice what this activity involves. By skimming the text and focusing upon a key idea in the story before even reading it, your students are engaging in an excellent prereading activity that fits a variety of strategies; also, they are incorporating writing skills into their reading instruction.

• Select a brief paragraph from the text and break each of the sentences down into sets of shorter ones to be combined. Cluster the sets. Have the students combine each set to generate the original paragraph.

Use the same procedure employed in the previous activity.

• Write a brief paragraph of short, choppy sentences. Relate this paragraph to the theme or topic of the text. Ask students to improve your paragraph by combining sentences in various ways. Discuss this paragraph and its contents in terms of the text to be read.

• After students have had some experience combining sentences, reverse the process. Have them select sentences from the text or some that they have written; have them break down the sentences into sets of short, choppy ones. Ask them to exchange with other students and try to combine those prepared by their classmates. Follow with discussions of the results, tying these to the text.

Keep the following in mind:

1. Do sentence-combining on a regular basis (once or twice a week).
2. Keep sentence-combining activities brief. They can easily become drill-like if overdone.
3. As much as possible, use text that students will be reading and tie your discussion to the text.
4. Use a variety of sentence-combining types, e.g., open, cued, and slotted.
5. After students have experience, reverse the process.
6. Capitalize upon the opportunities for paired activities with sentence-combining, in addition to class discussion.

Teaching the Logical Structure of Sentences

Although there is some correspondence between the grammatical structure of sentences and their logical structure, that correspondence is not one-to-one. Semantics generally and meanings of individual key words play more predominant roles in logical structure. For example, consider the difference between the following two sentences, which are quite similar grammatically:

1. If the car runs out of gasoline, it will stop running.
2. Only if the car runs out of gasoline will it stop running.

The word *only* plays a major role in changing the meaning of the second sentence. The first states a sufficient condition. Running out of gasoline is sufficient to make the car stop. The second sentence asserts a necessary condition that must exist for the car to stop running. A bit absurd, to say the least, since we know that other things can cause a car to stop as well.

Readers of expository text, especially, need to be aware of the different ways we have of asserting ideas with logical statements. In particular, if-then and either-or assertions can be quite troublesome; yet they are perhaps the most critical assertion statements for the reader to master to effectively comprehend expository text.

In addition, the use of negatives can complicate the logical, as well as the grammatical, complexity of statements in expository text. Consider the following, for example:

1. If taxes are increased, we shall not have a growth economy.
2. If taxes are not increased, we shall have a growth economy.
3. If taxes are not increased, we shall not have a growth economy.

4. If taxes are increased, we shall have a growth economy.
5. If we do not have a growth economy, the taxes have been increased.
6. If we do have a growth economy, the taxes have not been increased.

Forgetting the truth about the relationship between tax increases and growth economies, and considering only the similarity in meaning between these assertions, we can see that the presence of negatives can make statements complex, especially in if-then assertions. Readers of expository text need to be aware of these complexities and the general logical rules which govern their presence in statements of exposition.

A few points of importance regarding this type of logical expression in text are:

1. Antecedents and consequents in if-then statements are not reciprocal. That is, you cannot flip the *if* clause and the *then* clause around as they are written without destroying the original meaning, e.g., "If you study, then you will pass" does *not* mean the same thing as "If you passed, then you studied," even if the latter happens to be true.

2. Antecedents and consequents in if-then statements can be flipped if each is negated in the process. For example, "If you study, then you will pass" rotated and negated gives the logically equivalent "If you do not pass, then you did not study."

3. If-then statements can be restated as logically equivalent either-or statements by negating the *If* clause and changing the If-then structure to Either-or. For example, "If the bill passes, the middle class will suffer" is logically equivalent to "Either the bill does not pass, or the middle class will suffer."

4. Although double negation in sentences does not always add up to a positive, it can. "I still yet don't want no mustard" doesn't mean that I want some mustard. However, if I say, "It is not the case that I do not care for any mustard," I have just told you—in rather pretentious fashion—that I would like to have some mustard.

5. Although if-then statements are the most obvious form to express cause-effect within sentences, there are a variety of other cause-effect assertions that are roughly equivalent to if-then statements. For example:
   a. You hit me and I'll tell my mommy! (If you hit me, then I'll tell my mommy.)
   b. Whenever stagnated highs are present, we have nice weather. (If you have stagnated highs, then you have nice weather.)
   c. You need only to work hard to get ahead in the world. (If you work hard, then you will get ahead in the world.)

Although in formal logic, we may see all or most cause-effect assertions formalized as if-then or either-or statements, in normal, informal expository text, readers are much more likely to meet language such as that above. Readers need to recognize it and the cause-effect relationships that are being asserted by the author.

Activities

The following ideas can be helpful in designing activities to teach some of these important intra-sentence, logical relationships.

• Find logical statements in the text, i.e., if-then statements, to discuss with students. For example, what can be inferred from a statement such as, "If the bill passes and inflation continues low, then the chances for having a growth economy are very good"? Is this conditional derived from other data? Does it state necessary or sufficient conditions? What does it preclude? What does it leave as a possibility? As a probability?

• Have students write their own if-then assertions and think of logically equivalent ways to state them, e.g., using negatives or changing to either-or statements.

• In their text, have students search for if-then assertions in logical statement form other than the if-then form, i.e., cause-effect statements that do not use the words *if* or *then*.*

• Have students make up cause-effect assertions without using the words *if-then*. See how many different ways it can be done.

• Have students do word counts of different logical terms used in a text they are reading, e.g., words such as *if, only, because, since, whenever, in order for, in spite of the fact that, although, either-or, provided,* and so on. Ask them to restate these sentences as if-then assertions.

All of these activities require students to analyze the text closely—word-for-word, in fact—which also helps them understand text structure. A good deal of reading comprehension comes from skimming, looking for main ideas, getting the gist, keying general background knowledge and experience into the general direction of the text, and so on. While many of the strategies, techniques, and activities discussed in previous chapters were designed to do this, close analysis makes an important contribution to reading comprehension as well.

Inter-Sentence Structures: Expository and Narrative

Just as sentences have internal grammatical and logical structure that the reader must master, inter-sentence units of discourse—namely paragraphs and multiple-paragraph passages—have internal structure which the reader must also master. Unfortunately, we have a great deal yet to learn about the nature of this structure. (We know much more about sentence structure, although we can learn more there as well.)

---

* In English we often omit the word *then* in if-then statements. For example, "If the weather is nice, we'll have a picnic" rather than "If the weather is nice, then we shall have a picnic."

We have learned enough about inter-sentence structure to know that it varies, with different forms of text, in grammar, vocabulary, logic, and overall style. Consider the following examples:

> Reading instruction can be boring. Aspects of the standard reading lesson are monotonous. Many of the tasks assigned to children in the name of reading are drudgery. Thus, it is not surprising that in one study, for instance, interviews with a sample of poor, black children reading a year above grade level indicated that most liked to read, but few liked the activities called "reading" in the school.
>
> R.C. Anderson, et al.
> *Becoming a Nation of Readers*

> Permission to make shipments overseas come in a number of different colors and forms, ranging from a basic license which applies to a limited number of shipment types to more specialized ones. There are also "government reviewed" licenses which are subject to federal agency review. The agency involved determines the review process for that particular license. The arms exportation license is one example of this type of license where the national security agencies must grant approval.
>
> Robert Ludlum, *The Acquitaine Progresson*

The first paragraph is expository; the second is narrative. They represent the two basic forms (which have variations) that expository writing takes.

The first opens with a direct thesis assertion; the remaining sentences of the paragraph are designed to support the assertion. In fact, we have an opening topic sentence, followed by two support statements and a final, specific example intended to illustrate or support the main contention of the paragraph.

The second paragraph opens with what seems to be a thesis assertion. However, as we read on, it is clear that it is a general descriptor followed by sentences that are more specific, i.e., less abstract, in character.

After studying a quantity of narrative writing, Frances Christensen (1965) described its text structure as an abstraction-level movement, rather than a support of thesis assertion.

We can illustrate this by rewriting the Ludlum paragraph and tracking the abstraction-level movement by indenting, where an indented sentence or sentence part is less abstract than that indented; and with numbers, where higher numbers represent less abstract levels of representation. The paragraph looks this way:

1. Permission to make shipments overseas come in a number of different colors and forms,
   2. ranging from a basic license which applies to a limited number of shipment types
      3. to more specialized ones.

    2.   There are also "government reviewed" licenses which are subject to federal agency review.

        3.   The agency involved determines the review process for that particular license.

            4.   The arms exportation license is one example of this type of license where the national security agencies must grant approval.

Viewed this way, the paragraph becomes a two-part construction, each with three levels of abstraction and each reflecting the same direction of abstraction-level movement (even though the second part has slightly different abstraction levels).

Although this paragraph is obviously more syntactically advanced, similar structural patterns can be seen in less sophisticated narrative. For example:

1.   Since they were all Fred,

    2.   each one had a bundle of money bigger than a house,

        3.   in a wagon twice as big as a house,

            4.   pulled by two horses as big as barns.

J. Williams, "One Big Wish," in the
Economy Reading Series, *Spring Flight*,
Level 2, 1986, p. 119

As we examine longer passages of exposition and narration, we find that each reflects attributes which essentially are extensions of what we found in the paragraph-length text.

Expository text tends to follow one of two general patterns. If expository text is primarily persuasive or argumentative, it moves from *claim* (usually an initial opening thesis statement, which is developed in the first paragraph) to *support* or *development* (including appropriate specific examples or necessary detail to support the initial thesis) to *conclusion* (which can be a single statement in the last paragraph of a passage or, more likely, oblique statements within that last paragraph).

Here is an abbreviated example:

> The first generalization is that *reading is a constructive process.* No text is completely self-explanatory. In interpreting a text, readers draw on their store of knowledge about the topic of the text. Readers use this prior knowledge to fill in the gaps in the message and to integrate the different pieces of information in the message. That is to say, readers "construct" the meaning. In the restaurant example, the reader is able to infer that Mary sat at a table, selected her meal from the menu, and was probably served by the attendant. Yet none of this information is expressly mentioned in the text. These details are constructed from the reader's other knowledge of restaurants.

The meaning constructed from the same text can vary greatly among people because of differences in the knowledge they possess. Sometimes people do not have enough knowledge to understand a text, or they may have knowledge that they do not use fully. Variations in interpretation often arise because people have different conceptions about the topic than the author supposed.

R.C. Anderson, et al.
Becoming a Nation of Readers

(The third paragraph of this passage cites specific research to show that children who knew more about a specific subject did better on a reading test when reading a text about that subject than did children without the prior knowledge. In other words, this was a specific supporting detail for the original thesis.)

In the above example italics effectively highlight the thesis assertion. Each of the paragraphs provides support generalizations, with specific detail worked in for credibility and substantiation. Although the concluding paragraph does not appear here, it contains an oblique conclusion—the author assumes that the reader can infer the conclusion from the strength of the argument and the evidence offered.

If the expository text is primarily descriptive and explanatory (as in newspaper articles), its movement differs from that of persuasive text. The first paragraph essentially summarizes the entire content—in case the reader is in a hurry. The following paragraphs provide supporting detail and specifics, while the conclusion appears in the final paragraph. This text is simple and direct, it moves from *overview* to *detail* to *conclusion*. For example:

TERRORIST ATTACK LEAVES 24 DEAD
IN SYNAGOGUE

ISTANBUL, Turkey—Two Arab terrorists stormed Istanbul's main synagogue Saturday, killing 21 worshipers and wounding many others with machine guns before killing themselves.

The gunmen came in through the main door, locking it after them. They then sprayed the congregation with bullets while screaming in Arabic at the group.

Police indicated that the terrorists pulled the pins on grenades as authorities stormed the building, killing themselves and wounding many others in the vicinity.

Authorities are investigating in order to determine the source of the attack and the extent of the damage.

The first paragraph contains the gist of the article. The body of the article is concerned with detail, and the last paragraph suggests next steps—a form of conclusion typical in reportive text.

If the text is narrative, it is simpler than expository on the one hand, and more complex on the other. With longer (and well-written) narrative text, the abstraction-level movement is quite irregular. It does not always move from more to less abstract as in the Ludlum excerpt; often it moves in the opposite direction, from less to more abstract. For example:

    4. As if with the grace of a turtle,
    3. lurching awkwardly down the road,
    2. looking huge beyond its real size,
    1. the old truck slowly neared the crowd.

Usually, better narrative contains an ongoing mixture of each movement. Occasionally there are runs, as in the above example where detailed description moves in one direction for awhile before changing. On some occasions the writer uses extended parallelism to create syntactic units of the same abstraction level, for example:

    2. Worry over the house,
    2. concern about the mother,
    2. pressure at work,
    2. problems with the kids,
    1. all had finally taken their toll on Henry.

However, it is that general in-and-out movement of the text that makes narrative exciting and appealing.

    Readers need to be consciously aware of how authors use text structure for purpose and effect and that this varies with expository and narrative text. Beginning in the early grades students should be exposed to both narrative and expository text, with exposure to exposition increasing as they enter the intermediate grades. Instruction should include examination of the basic patterns in exposition and the abstraction-level movement in narration.

Activities

    ● Present the two basic expository text patterns to the class in outline form with examples of each. Ask them to find examples of each in their textbook or basal reader.

    ● In their notebooks have students document examples of expository and narrative text that they find outside the classroom over a period of several days. Discuss the sources of their examples.

    ● Teach the students a simplified outline using indents and numbers to identify abstraction levels in a narrative passage. Give them samples of narrative and have them rewrite the samples using the outline to indicate abstraction-level movement.

You can precede and follow this with class presentations on an overhead projector. Give the class samples of narrative text and, as a group, write the outline on a transparency. Move to more complex and lengthy passages as students acquire the skill.

● Have students write sample narrative passages and exchange them with other students. Ask each student to outline his or her classmate's passage using the narrative outline. Have them discuss the work of each.

● Use the front page of a newspaper to identify descriptive or explanatory expository text (summary/detailed support/conclusion or next steps). Ask students to identify each of the components in an article.

Do the same for persuasive exposition. The editorial page of the same newspaper can be an excellent resource.

Text Cohesion

Authors use a variety of devices and techniques to make their text well-organized and consistently developed. Transitional sentences are often used at the end of a paragraph to prepare the reader for the next paragraph. Transition words are used in key parts of a text; words such as *however, then, soon, later, after,* and so on. Placed in key sentences—usually in the beginning or near the very end of a paragraph—these words key the reader to a shift in events or a continuation of events, if that is desired.

However, most of these devices or techniques are stylistic and organizational. They are consciously chosen by the author out of a small range of linguistic options available, and their placement in the text is selective and quite limited. Fortunately, authors have recourse to other means.

It is in the inherent nature of the structure and semantic character of language itself that text finds coherence—that text coheres, or binds itself to itself. Effective writers and readers are consciously aware of these features; the most effective writers and readers consciously employ their knowledge of text coherence features to enrich their writing and reading.

What are some of these cohesive forms and types? One type is *anaphoric. Anaphora* is a technical term which means "backward reference of a word or phrase in text." Related technical terms are *cataphora* and *exophora.* A cataphoric relationship of terms is "forward referencing," while an exophoric relationship is "generalized or generic referencing." The use of pronouns affords the most common means for indicating referencing directions, which is known as pronominal referencing. For example:

1. John ate the apple quickly. *He* was in a hurry. (Anaphoric relationship between the pronoun *he* and the referent *John;* the pronoun refers back to an earlier-established referent.)
2. *It* was quiet while slowly creeping through the undergrowth; the

big cat was searching carefully for prey. (Cataphoric relationship between the pronoun *it* and the referent cat; the pronoun is used *prior* to its referent.)

3. *It* doesn't seem to make much difference what we do. (Exophoric relationship; the pronoun *it* has no specific referent identifiable in the text.)

Of these three cohesive forms, probably the most commonly employed is the anaphoric. Halladay and Hasan (1976) identify four important types of anaphoric ties:

1. *Referential Cohesive Ties:* Words used to refer to something else rather than being interpreted in their own right.

   Example: *Bill* was proud of *his* new fishing rod and reel. *His* grandfather had given it to *him* for *his* birthday. (personal reference)

2. *Substitution Cohesive Ties*: A word is replaced by another one.

   Example: This fishing *line* is not strong enough. I must get a heavier *one*. (nominal substitution)

   Example: Shall I put the fish on the stringer? Please *do*, as soon as possible. (verbal substitution)

   Example: *Will we catch lots of fish?* Dad says *so*. (clausal substitution)

3. *Ellipsis*: A word is omitted. Substitution and ellipsis are essentially the same process; however, with ellipsis the word is replaced by nothing.

   Example: Here are the fish I caught. Where are yours (fish)? (nominal ellipsis)

   Example: Have you been fishing? Yes, I have (been fishing). (verbal ellipsis)

   Example: Who taught you to cast so well? Dad did (taught me to cast so well). (clausal ellipsis)

4. *Lexical Cohesion:* Cohesive effect is achieved by using related vocabulary, namely *collocates*.

   Example: Bill fell into the *lake* while fishing. The *water* was very deep. (lexical reiteration)

   Example: Bill baited the *hook* quickly. Then he dropped the *line* into the *water*. (lexical collocation)

When you examine any expository or narrative text, the extent to which the author uses anaphoric relationships to bind text together becomes obvious. Read this brief passage, for example:

> "How strange it is that I did not see the flowers!"
>
> The nearer she approached the shrub, the more attractive it looked. It bore above a hundred flowers of the most brilliant hues, and each different from the others. But there was a deep, glossy lustre on the leaves, and on the petals of the flowers, that made Proserpina doubt whether they might not be poisonous.

> Nathaniel Hawthorne, "The Pomegranate Seeds,"
> in the Economy Reading Series, *Harvest
> Moon*, Level 8, 1986

Notice how anaphoric relationships cement this text together. As passages become longer, the distance between anaphoric ties can lengthen. It is not uncommon for the reader to refer back as far as four or five paragraphs to locate a pronominal or collocational referent established by the author. Of course, the greater the distance between anaphora and their referents, the more complex comprehension becomes and the more demanding.

Wide and extensive reading provides the reader with probably the best single way to practice spotting cohesive ties and tie patterns. Although this is necessary for effective comprehension, it is not likely to be *sufficient* for effective comprehension.

Learners also need direct instruction in text structure, where cohesion is highlighted. The following activities and techniques can be helpful at a variety of grades to focus developing readers upon these important linguistic devices.

Techniques and Activities

● Provide students with the Halladay/Hasan categories of anaphoric forms and devices, with appropriate examples of each. (These categories can be modified to adjust for grade level.) Provide ample class discussion,with a range of examples to give students some background in the concept of cohesion.

Select a brief passage of text from their reading and format it on a handout such as the following:

The last word ended in a long bleat, so like a sheep that Alice quite started (1). She looked at the Queen, who seemed to have suddenly wrapped herself up in wool (2). Alice rubbed her eyes, and looked again (3). She couldn't make out what had happened at all (4). Was she in a shop (5)? And, was that really—was it really a sheep that was sitting on the other side of the counter (6)? Rub as she would, she could make nothing more of it (7).

SENTENCE NUMBER	COHESION TERM	REFERENT
1		
2		
3		
4		

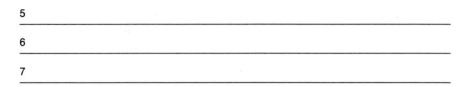

Have your students identify the anaphora and their referents in each sentence. The anaphora and referents should be written in the appropriate places in columns opposite the sentence number in which they appear. It is possible to have the same referents used more than once.

To provide more clues you can type the anaphora, or referents, or both in capitals or boldface on the handouts.

After students have completed the handout, discuss their results in class. Talk about the different results (if any) and ask students to explain their choices whenever possible.

● Selectively cloze text with blank spaces slotted into the position of anaphora or referents—separate activities can focus upon each. For example:

> The hunter slowly moved into the forest. __(He)__ peered into the undergrowth wondering about __(his)__ ammunition supply. Would __(it)__ be enough in case the big cat showed? __(It)__ had escaped the hunter on __(his)__ last trip __(here)__ .

Passages pulled from students' textbooks or basal readers are excellent. During prereading these can be used to introduce the students to the content or theme of the text. They can check their clozing with the words actually used by the author. Discussion can follow on the appropriateness of each.

With lengthier passages to be clozed, you can increase the distance between the anaphora and referents, thus making that task more difficult. Further, once readers understand how difficult it is to make connections between anaphora and distant referents, they can more readily see how text becomes ambiguous and how best to deal with it. As distance between referential ties increases, the number of intervening possible referents also increases, the reader must search amongst context clues to establish the proper connections.

● Provide students with a handout of a passage of text. Have them circle the anaphora and referents; then have them use arrows to illustrate the anaphoric relation and direction of reference. For example:

The Mazamas instituted a program of annual outings, beginning with a trip to Crater Lake in 1896. These were large undertakings. Many people went, some to climb, some not, but all to enjoy the mountains. After the Crater Lake trip the group established a habit of visiting the Northwest's large volcanoes Mounts Rainier, Adams, Jefferson, Hood, the Three Sisters and Shasta in the next decade. They chose Mount Baker as the object of their annual outing in 1906.

John Miles, *Koma Kulshan: The Story of Mt. Baker*

As a variation, have them select passages, write them down, and circle and arrow the anaphoric relationships. Have students exchange those efforts and score each other's papers.

● For a specific text, design *Wh* questions that focus on anaphoric relationships. For example, using the John Miles text, you might ask the following questions:

Who instituted the trips?

To what does the word *these* in the second sentence refer?

In the last sentence, what does *object* refer to?

● Present students with a passage of contrived text that is devoid of pronouns but instead includes repeated noun phrases; the redundancy will stand out. Have your students rewrite the passage by employing appropriate pronouns or collocates. For example:

John knew that John needed to practice to be a good player, so John worked hard. John's practice showed the result of John's efforts, and John was soon rewarded by John's coach. John made the first team and John was proud of John's efforts.

You can vary this activity by overusing pronouns instead, so that the text becomes ambiguous; the pronoun reference becomes confused as new potential referents are introduced.

● You can also modify this activity to focus upon *collocational referencing*, the use of related terms in a given text or a passage.

The assumptive bases of semantic mapping, which we discussed earlier in this book, are rooted in what we know about collocates and their referencing in text. Certain label words tend to attract families of like-related words within their text domains. Where semantic mapping has been used as a prereading technique, activities such as those discussed here can be used during the reading and postreading phases to serve as a check on the earlier word maps.

It must be kept in mind that the various techniques and activities discussed in this chapter are neither as detailed as they could be nor as comprehensive in number as they might be. They are instead chosen to illustrate a selection of solid, workable ideas that can be modified or altered in a number of ways to provide the greatest range of potential applicability. They can be slotted into a number of teaching strategies in a range of reading program philosophies.

Perhaps the most important attribute of these activities is that they all require the learner to pursue the text closely and analytically. They force one to attend to the structure of language and the structure of text types and purposes. Because many of our other strategies and techniques do not require such rigorous analysis, this dimension should not be forgotten, nor given stepchild status in the reading program.

Good readers attend to their minds, to the author's mind, *and* to the structure of the text being addressed.

ADDITIONAL SELECTED READINGS

BAUMANN, J. AND JOHNSON, D. (Eds.). (1984). *Reading instruction and the beginning teacher.* Minneapolis: Burgess.

DEVINE, T. (1986). *Teaching reading comprehension: From theory to practice.* Boston: Allyn and Bacon.

HARNADEK, A. (1976). *Critical thinking.* Pacific Grove, Calif.: Midwest Publications.

IRWIN, J. W. (1986). *Teaching reading comprehension processes.* Englewood Cliffs, N.J.: Prentice-Hall.

IRWIN, J. W. (Ed.). (1986). *Understanding and teaching cohesion comprehension.* Newark, Dela.: IRA.

KLEIN, M. (1987). Sentence and paragraph building in the language arts. In C. Personke and D. Johnson (Eds.), *Language arts and the beginning teacher.* Englewood Cliffs, N.J.: Prentice-Hall.

MASON, J. AND AU, K. (1986). *Reading instruction for today.* Glenview, Ill.: Scott, Foresman.

REFERENCES

ANDERSON, R. ET AL. (Eds.). (1985). *Becoming a nation of readers.* Urbana, Ill.: Center for the Study of Reading, University of Illinois.

CHRISTENSEN, F. (1965). A generative rhetoric of the sentence. *College Composition and Communication, 14,* 155–161.

COMBS, W. (1977). Sentence-combining aids reading comprehension. *Journal of Reading,* (Oct.) 18–24.

HALLIDAY, M.A.K. AND HASAN, R. (1976) *Cohesion in English.* London: Longman, 336.

MATTEONI, L. (1986). *Economy reading series.* Oklahoma City, Okla.: McGraw-Hill.

MILES, J. (1984). *Koma Kulshan: The story of Mt. Baker.* Seattle: The Mountaineers.

7

Basal Readers

A POWERFUL FORCE

Over the years basal reading programs have been a major area of debate for reading educators. Many assert that the readers are incomplete, too restrictive, and premised too heavily upon a reading-as-skills-acquisition perspective. They too narrowly define the range of techniques and activities the teacher can use, and they dictate a structured ordering of instruction that allows for no individualization or recognition of individual differences in learners.

Supporters of basal reading programs argue just as substantially that these programs provide a basic reading curriculum with a scope and sequence that enables schools to implement and maintain a systematic content that assures some degree of accountability. Basals, they say, are not at fault for the most part. They provide complete reading instruction guidance and allow the teacher time for the myriad other teaching and non-teaching tasks to be faced in the course of a day.

As with most things in life, there is some value in each of the arguments. Regardless of one's own feelings, however, basal programs represent a powerful instructional force in our schools. Any consideration of the role of basal readers in reading comprehension and reading vocabulary instruction must derive from an examination of the overall role of the basal, so some understanding of its nature and function must come first.

Of the various debates and arguments about basal readers that dominate the scene, many choose to ignore one very fundamental point: The overwhelming majority of schools in this country rely heavily upon them. Some estimate that as many as 98% or more of the schools use the basal as their basic reading program. The basal reader is a part of our educational life and it is not likely to disappear from the scene in the foreseeable future. Therefore, it makes sense to do the best we can to make the basal as complete and as strong as possible. We should also do our best to see that teachers and curriculum people know how to most effectively use the material produced by commercial publishers.

Overview of Basal Reading Programs

Typically, a basal reading program is a K–8 or sometimes a K–6 series of student readers containing a selection of stories, poems, plays, and nonfiction. Although some selections are original, most are written by professional authors—sometimes for the reading series itself, other times for other publications and permission is granted for use of the material in the basal series. Readers for upper grade levels often contain excerpts from longer works, such as novels.

A second component is the teacher's guide or, as it is sometimes called, the teacher's edition. This volume, which accompanies each grade or series level, provides the detailed lessons and instructions on use of the student text. The teacher's guide typically contains in-depth directions on how to teach each selection and provides word-by-word narrative and detailed questions to ask at various points in the reading.

A third component is the student workbook or workbooks. This component varies considerably from publisher to publisher. Most have more than one workbook available for students. Sometimes these are called *activity books* or *skill books*, since the term *workbook* has developed so many negative connotations over the years. The role of these books also can vary. They might be designed to reinforce particular skills the program is built upon, or they might be designed for remedial purposes or for extended application purposes. Some programs also include a range of duplicating masters in addition to the workbooks. These too can serve different roles, depending upon the program.

A fourth component is the testing and management system that accompanies the program. Here also programs vary. Some provide tests designed to serve in assessment roles, with separate tests for diagnostic purposes. Some advocate pretesting and post-testing. Most employ a standardized test format. Often schools use the tests according to the district testing policy, so publishers must meet the needs of a variety of testing approaches.

Management is usually built around diagnostic testing, although most programs include recommendations for grouping and instruction based upon less formal assessment as well.

A fifth component of most basal reading programs is usually called the *teacher's resource manual*. This is a relatively new component in basals. Typically formatted in a three-ring binder, this document contains resource materials for the teacher ranging from duplicating masters for classroom use to copies of professional articles or monographs on reading instruction prepared by the series' authors and others in the reading field. The manual appears increasingly like an in-service tool for teachers. Its role is to supplement the teacher's guide that contains instructions on teaching lessons.

A sixth component is in the area of computers. Currently, most of the technology included in basal reading programs focuses upon the use of software for testing and management. Although most publishers are working on the development of various supplemental software components to be used as adjuncts to their basals, there is little instructional software accompanying specific reading programs other than what is available from supplementary publishers (which they often correlate with basal programs).

In addition to these six standard components, most programs contain a variety of other supplemental materials from picture cards to puppets to take-home letters for parents, and so on.

Although there is a considerable volume of materials that can be purchased for each student, the heart of the basal continues to be the teacher's guide. As one major publisher asserted, "We do not publish reading programs for children. We publish reading programs for teachers. If they do not use the materials properly, then it makes no difference what else we do." And, it is in the teacher's guide that any debate over basal use often centers—there and in the beginning stories of the preprimers and primers.

Features of Basal Reading Programs

Controlled Vocabulary

In the early portions of the program, most basals provide gradual introduction of new words and some plan for incorporating those new words in later lessons. The argument for this approach is that research suggests learners can be overwhelmed with the introduction of too many new words at once. In addition, initial instruction in word attack usually presupposes some plan for systematically teaching phoneme/grapheme relationships without the instruction being confounded by too many new words, where concept load begins to interfere.

Those who are critical of this approach argue that this requires the early stories to be written in a stilted style that is unlike either the oral language the child brings to school or the language of text found in most reading materials. Many language-experience advocates, for example, initially prefer to transcribe stories from the oral language of the learner to reflect the natural language of the beginning reader.

Skill-Centered Approach

Most basal programs articulate a scope and sequence of reading skills in the various areas of reading—word attack, comprehension, vocabulary, study skills, literary skills, and so on. In fact, the scopes of reading comprehension skills found in the various basals are quite similar. They do differ in their sequence, especially in the subskill sets, or categories, that most employ. Supporters feel that this allows effective articulation and common direction for the entire reading program.

Critics suggest that the contemporary research emphasizes the importance of the reading process and suggests that reading acquisition is not affected by ordering hierarchies of skills and subskills in reading programs.

Lesson Plan Format

Teacher's guides lay out detailed plans for each lesson with step-by-step instructions. Although the lesson format varies from program to program, a typical lesson begins with a statement of objectives and identification of preselection vocabulary, with recommended steps for teaching the vocabulary. More recent programs then include a section entitled "Building Background Knowledge" or something similar. Here teachers are led through the steps of encouraging learners, primarily through questioning, to focus upon key ideas that they can relate from their personal backgrounds to the selection to be read. This is followed with suggested discussion questions and, finally, suggested postreading or extension activities.

Proponents indicate that this sort of step-by-step process is important to assure adequate treatment of key reading skills and that elementary grade teachers—especially beginning teachers—need the detailed direction. It considerably reduces the pressure of preparing lessons.

Critics say that this sort of lock-step arrangement stifles creativity and is overly redundant. They also point out that the standard lesson format does not take into account the differences in various kinds of text, i.e., poetry, nonfiction, and so on, and that it does not allow for the range of student abilities that exists in most reading classes.

Testing

Tests that accompany the basal program focus upon the skills which define the content of the instruction. Tests are typically organized around units in the text and include subtests which address skills in the areas of word attack, comprehension, vocabulary, and so on. According to the publishers, these tests allow the teacher to diagnose, monitor, and assess the reading achievement of all the learners, thus providing a documented set of data to use when deciding how to individualize instruction. In addition, of course, the district has a means of measuring reading achievement through the course of the year—an important point in an age of educational accountability.

Critics say there is too much testing—so much, in fact, that teachers could spend the majority of their time testing. Further, critics add, the tests are often of poor quality. Because test development, including the technical steps of validating the contents and establishing reliability, is so costly and time consuming, publishers release the tests with the other basal materials before knowing if the contents are valid and reliable.

The Basal Approach to Reading Comprehension

Most basals that have been developed in the past four or five years commit significant portions of their content to instruction in comprehension. Also, they begin this instruction much earlier, even in the initial stages of primary-grade instruction. There are some exceptions. Some programs still are touted as *phonics first* programs, and it would be proper to say that most of the initial focus in the primary grades, at least, is upon word attack.

Comprehension and reading vocabulary are usually treated as two different strands, or components, within the basal text.

Since most basals do not use very precise definitions of the instructional terms *strategy* and *technique*, it is difficult to ascribe particular approaches to particular programs using these terms. It is perhaps enough to note that all basal programs purport to have comprehension strategies designed to improve one's understanding of what one reads. For the most part, these strategies are bound up in the basal's use of questioning.

The Role of Questioning

There are some commonalities in the questioning approaches used by the various basal readers. For example, all the contemporary reading programs categorize questions by some sort of cognitive taxonomy. The taxonomies employed are usually a simplified version of Bloom, Barrett, or Sanders, although currently there is some interest in incorporating other taxonomic schemes. It is reasonable to assume that in the next few years most new reading programs will attend closely to story grammars and use one or more of these as an outline for designing questions for fictional text. Interest in nonfiction models such as Bonnie Armbruster's is likely to lead to increased use of questioning strategies and techniques employing alternative approaches.

It is important to note, however, that many of the newer models of processing, such as those referred to in this book are more complex than even the earlier Bloom work. Many implicitly if not explicitly demand formulation of extended questioning strategies built upon the models, rather than the use of the model as only a categorizing system for a variety of questions or question types. In fact, one problem with some contemporary reading basals is their tendency to simply ask a variety of questions at the end of a selection that have been categorized by some taxonomy to assure the teacher that there is a range of levels. Unfortunately, as we noted earlier in this book, simply plying the taxonomic range is not likely to improve reading comprehension abilities significantly. Fortunately, fewer and fewer programs do only that.

There are some differences in how various programs establish categories of questions and then use them in the teacher's guide. For example, Macmillan SERIES R (1986) treats comprehension skills that are familiar in most programs—cause-effect, predicting outcomes, paraphrasing, sequencing, main-ideas detection, and so on. However, they establish four fundamental categories (literal comprehension, interpretive thinking, critical thinking, and creative thinking) for the design of their questions. The use of the term *thinking* in their categories and the inclusion of attention to notions such as *syllogisms* in their scope and sequence suggest that their program intends to push for the development of thinking.

Other programs, such as Heath (1986), choose to continue with categories such as literal versus interpretive versus applied comprehension questions.

The ECONOMY READING SERIES (1986) uses a somewhat unusual approach, asking a higher-level, *gist* question to focus the learner's attention on the most important idea or ideas of the text. The gist question is then followed by *probe* questions which require the reader to use key data or support necessary for inferring the higher-level question.

Some, such as the ECONOMY READING SERIES, attempt to use questioning in prereading to activate or build background knowledge for the reading. Unfortunately, many of the older programs do not attend to the prereading phase as thoroughly as they should, if they do at all.

Certainly not enough of any of the programs attend to design of questioning strategies that link questions asked during the prereading to those asked during the reading and after the reading of the text.

An overall review of the treatment of comprehension development through questioning in contemporary basal reading programs reveals:

1. Basals have improved significantly in using a variety of levels of questions in the development of their questioning approaches.
2. Basals have done some interesting things in redesigning various categories to focus the reader's attention upon particular kinds of thinking.

3. Basals have attempted to incorporate some of the contemporary research in reading comprehension into the design of their questioning approaches.

4. Basal reading programs need to formulate specific questioning strategies that allow for greater versatility, flexibility, and variety so that the specific strategy chosen can be fitted to the type of text and the needs of the students in a given instructional context.

5. Basal reading programs need to continue to develop questioning approaches that enable the learner to see the relationship between what was discussed prior to the reading and what was discussed after the reading.

6. Basal reading programs need to provide a greater range of possible *scenarios* of questions and discussion based upon feedback provided by the students and the various directions that questioning can take based upon that feedback.

Writing and Metacognition

Advocates of a language experience approach to teaching reading, advocates of whole language approaches, advocates of an integrated language arts/reading approach, and those who see a need for attention to metacognitive development have been major critics of the basal reader. Many of these critics and other educators who favor a more comprehensive approach to the development of literacy, rather than the older notion of *reading*, suggest that basals largely isolate reading skills and processes from the other important literacy domains.

Examination of contemporary programs, however, suggests that although there is much yet to be done in this area, publishers of basal reading programs have attempted to address a number of these ideas. Most programs now, for example, include writing as an ongoing part of the instructional plan; however, most of that writing is done during the pre-reading period or after the reading has been completed. There is still a need to build the writing process into the instruction so that it is not merely an adjunct, but is integral. Some of the ideas discussed earlier in this volume address this idea to some extent.

As with writing, basals have not incorporated the ideas in metacognition. Certainly, any instruction in study skills represents an excellent opportunity to address this area of need. In addition, there are a variety of ways to use metacognitive ideas on a daily basis as part of the normal instruction in reading.

Currently, we are in a decade of strong advocacy for a more comprehensive approach to literacy development. Since the mid-1970s, when interest in early writing acquisition followed on the heels of a decade of significant research in oral language acquisition, there has been a constant, if not always totally endorsed, move to redefine our conception of what it means to be literate on the one hand, and how we acquire that literacy on the other.

Several of the larger states that use a state adoption process* have developed new frameworks and guidelines for decision-making on listing of new basal reading programs. Many of these new guidelines delineate criteria designed to encourage more integrated programs for reading and language arts instruction. The extent to which this trend will be reflected in different approaches to reading program development of all kinds remains to be seen.

On the whole, however, anyone who has seriously examined the content, format, and overall physical quality of contemporary basal reading programs compared with those of two decades ago will probably concur that there have been major improvements in all elements and features of most programs.

Incorporating the Basal into a Total Reading Program

When one considers the research and practice findings of the past decade, it becomes relatively easy to see why the complexities of the instructional task preclude overdependence upon any one book or set of materials. We know that what the teacher does before using any text materials plays a significant role in developing student comprehension. The situation is quite similar with reading vocabulary—especially the vocabulary that we want to see in learners' full-ownership dictionaries. To effectively learn reading vocabulary the student must be actively involved in oral language, in reading a wide variety of materials, and in the act of writing. In addition, these experiences should take place in both structured and unstructured learning environments. We know that effective reading comprehension requires a range of language interactions, both oral and written.

Therefore, readers should be perceived as directional but not directive. Most publishers recognize that their materials do not constitute a *total* reading program. The reading process is most effectively taught when the classroom teacher views basal readers as strong assists to the task. **The primary responsibility of the basal** in teaching comprehension and reading vocabulary **is to provide the critical parameters,** or central directional elements, but **not the perimeters**, the boundaries of instruction.

Even this responsibility, however, is significant. It means that the basal must provide critical information and direction for orchestrating instruction around important features of effective teaching. In doing so it must

*The term *state adoptions* refers to the more than twenty states in the United States that use a process of identifying a limited number of basal reading programs that school districts in that state may select from in order to receive state funding for the program. Normally, the process involves state committees and hearings where publishers who wish to compete present their programs. These committees then vote on those programs they feel are most appropriate for their state to choose from. Some states list five or so; others list more. In essence, being listed gives the publisher a license to sell in that state for that particular adoption cycle. Authorities both support and condemn the state adoption process.

incorporate the most important findings we have to date in comprehension and vocabulary research and practice.

Guidelines for Selecting and Using Basals

The following list of recommended criteria for the selection and use of basals in teaching comprehension and vocabulary essentially reviews key ideas presented elsewhere in this book. Notice that each criterion represents an underlying assumption about the effective teaching of reading.

CRITERIA FOR BASAL READING PROGRAMS

1. The student text contains a variety of text discourse types at each grade level—narrative, poetry, expository.
2. The student text provides text adjuncts, i.e., art work, photos, graphs, charts, and so on directly related to key ideas in the text and *not* simply as supplements to the text.
3. The student text provides prereading guides (advance organizers) as a matter of course for most selections in the text.
4. Any literature selections included in the student text that are excerpted from larger works are carefully chosen to reflect minimal suffering from acontextuality; adequate background and explanation is provided at the beginning of the text selection.
5. Preselection vocabulary is limited in number and related to important ideas in the text selection.
6. The teacher's guide clearly demarks lessons according to prereading, reading, and postreading with activities appropriate to each.
7. The teacher's guide provides suggestions for focused discussion during the prereading phase to activate and build background knowledge for learners.
8. The teacher's guide offers alternative approaches to the lesson *during* the reading, e.g., periodic question insertion.
9. The teacher's guide systematically incorporates writing into each lesson, both supplementally and integrally.
10. The teacher's guide, in the primary grades especially, provides guidance and ideas for teaching the *language of instruction*—the necessary metalanguage that children must master to benefit from the teacher's instruction.
11. The teacher's guide provides guidance and instruction in the teaching of study skills for use in all content areas.
12. The teacher's guide allows for alternative scenarios of lessons, depending upon the nature of the text and the objectives of the lesson.
13. The teacher's guide employs clear questioning strategies rather than simply using a questioning taxonomy for variety.
14. The teacher's guide uses story grammars and nonfiction models of question and discussion development for appropriate text.
15. The teacher's guide contains appropriate metacognitive techniques and activities on a regular basis.
16. The teacher's guide provides rich resources in background information necessary to the subject of the lesson and suggestions for incorporating a variety of materials outside the basal, for each lesson.

17. The teacher's guide encourages the integration of all language arts where appropriate by offering ideas for the teaching of comprehension and vocabulary.

18. The teacher's guide includes both direct instruction and indirect instruction, and both formal and informal models for the teaching of reading vocabulary.

19. The teacher's guide contains a straightforward, direct formal instruction strategy for teaching selected vocabulary.

20. The teacher's guide clearly indicates how new vocabulary maintenance is assured.

21. The teacher's guide focuses attention upon teaching learners the process of acquiring new reading vocabulary rather than just the acquisition of new words in the basal.

22. The teacher's guide builds comprehension and reading vocabulary instruction into the program in the earliest as well as in the later grades.

23. Student supplementary materials, i.e., activity books or workbooks, have a clear, focused role. One is remedial and coordinated with the diagnostic testing component, for example. Another focuses on extending the skills that were introduced.

24. There is an activity book that is not self-directional, i.e., students and the teacher use the material together.

25. There is a software component that correlates comprehension and reading vocabulary instruction for the computer with that in the basal text.

26. The basal provides a regular, ongoing in-service for the teacher, including professional materials, videos for use in-service and at workshops, and other appropriate materials.

REFERENCES

BAILEY, M.H. ET AL. (1986). *Heath american readers*, Lexington, Mass.: D.C. Heath.

DURR, W. ET AL. (1986). HOUGHTON MIFFLIN READING. Boston: Houghton Mifflin.

KLEIN, M., MATTEONI, L., SUCHER, F. AND WELCH, K. (1986). ECONOMY READING SERIES. Oklahoma City, Okla.: McGraw-Hill.

SMITH, C. AND ARNOLD, V. (1986), MACMILLAN SERIES R. New York: Macmillan.

8

Epilogue

This book has been concerned primarily with the objective of helping the teacher develop teaching strategies, techniques, and activities to teach comprehension and vocabulary more effectively. Throughout, the author has attempted to keep the teaching ideas relevant and practical—appropriate to a range of learning abilities and grade levels. I hope that they have not been reading-program-philosophy dependent, but rather, they have been the kinds of teaching ideas suitable for a variety of teaching contexts and conditions.

Along the way, if we have been lucky, some new things have been learned about reading and reading instruction that will translate into better, more effective teaching for you.

Before we part company, however, there are a few final points I think it important to keep in mind as a classroom teacher or as a curriculum person responsible in one way or another for the reading program in your school. In order to make this as concise and orderly as possible, I'll summarize these points and present them numerically, although order of presentation bears no necessary relationship to their importance. Some of these will simply be summaries of ideas presented directly in the previous text or indirectly by implication or statement. Others will be extensions of ideas I assume the reader has perceived as fundamental to the underlying rationale and philosophy of this book.

1. Reading acquisition and development is not the result of a simple accretion of discrete skills and concepts over a period of time regardless of manner or means of instruction. The reading process is far more complex than that. Development of the necessary processes of reading requires a variety of experiences, literacy-rich contexts and resources, opportunities to exploit all language-producing and language-consuming capacities in as many ways as possible, and a comprehensive reading program designed to recognize the importance of all of these.

2. Reading comprehension and reading vocabulary develop best in a comprehensive reading program that is premised upon a K–12 approach and in a reading program articulated throughout the grades and across all subject areas in all grades. Historically, reading instruction has been focused primarily in the K–6 grade range. Yet, some of the most lucrative opportunities to develop reading comprehension and vocabulary exist in later grades, after students have a richer array of background knowledge and are also more cognitively advanced. Much of the motivationally driven text exists in English, social studies, science, and other areas. The immediate and most functional need for comprehension and vocabulary exists there.

Although the individual classroom teacher cannot determine the extent to which a K–12 philosophy holds in an individual school district, individual teachers do make up the body of professionals who will determine its success or failure. The imperative to achieve the goals of a K–12 effort may, in fact, have its primary roots in the needs of the individual teacher.

3. Reading comprehension and vocabulary are most effectively developed in a reading program where the individual importance of the learner, the text, the context, and the interaction of all of these elements are capitalized upon. The reading program should reflect balance between *reader-driven* instruction and *text-driven* instruction. That balance is often best achieved through instruction based on interaction, where the teacher capitalizes upon the instructional context to translate each of the above dominant types into workable opportunites to enable the reader to merge the processes of each.

4. A solid oral language base is critical to the initial development of reading comprehension and vocabulary development. Oral language interaction remains the dominant means for the teacher to see to the interaction of reader and text and the processes of each. Good teaching techniques and activities are made so in most cases directly by the degree and *kind* of oral language interaction they invoke. Effective teaching strategies are *totally* dependent upon quality oral language interaction in the classroom.

The subtlety and complexity of that interaction during the reading lesson is substantial and cannot be underestimated. Its importance is directly related to that complexity. It is imperative that teachers develop a wide range of teaching abilities which enable them to exploit this area to make reading comprehension and vocabulary growth possible.

5. Effective teachers of reading comprehension and vocabulary see reading instruction as a three-phase process: prereading, reading, postreading. They design teaching strategies and techniques to fit that conception of instruction.

6. The driving force of a quality reading instruction program designed to develop comprehension and vocabulary is motivation and sense of need in learners. These derive from:

a. A teacher excited about reading and teaching it.
b. A positive learning environment.
c. Instructional strategies which are consistent and appropriate.
d. Techniques and activities which fit the strategies and bring reader and text together.
e. Quality literature which warrants being read.

Not necessarily difficult things to achieve, these. The results for our children warrant the effort.

Index